WITHDRAWN
FENG
SHUI
STRATEGIES FOR
BUSINESS SUCCESS

ALSO BY T. RAPHAEL SIMONS

Feng Shui Step by Step

FENG SHUI

STRATEGIES FOR BUSINESS SUCCESS

*Arranging Your Office for Success and Prosperity—
with Personalized Astrological Charts*

T. RAPHAEL SIMONS

THREE RIVERS PRESS
NEW YORK

Published by Three Rivers Press, a division of Crown Publishers, Inc., 201 East 50th Street, New York, New York 10022. Member of the Crown Publishing Group.

Random House, Inc. New York, Toronto, London, Sydney, Auckland
www.randomhouse.com

Three Rivers Press and colophon are trademarks of Crown Publishers, Inc.

Printed in the United States of America

Design by Julie Baker Schroeder

Library of Congress Cataloging-in-Publication Data
Simons, T. Raphael.
    Feng Shui strategies for business success : with personalized
astrological charts / T. Raphael Simons.
    (alk. paper)
    1. Feng Shui.   2. Astrology—Charts, diagrams, etc.   3. Success in
business.   I. Title.
BF1779.F4S566   1998
133.3'337—dc21   98-13490

ISBN 0-609-80230-5

10   9   8   7   6   5   4   3   2   1

First Edition

ACKNOWLEDGMENTS

To Kwan Ti, who inspired this book, I owe my gratitude. I also wish to express my heartfelt thanks to Zeng Xianwen for his excellent calligraphy; to Janet Aisawa for her valued insights; to Sandra Cousins for her kind interest and moral support; to Terry Lee, who taught me the authentic practice of feng shui; to the Reverend Yamamoto, who taught me the lucky star system; to Sue Herner, my agent, for her encouragement and generous spirit; to Carol Southern, my editor, whose sense of artistry is an inspiration; to my brilliant copy editor, Susan Brown; to everyone at Potter/Crown who helped to bring this book to fruition—Annetta Hanna, Camille Smith, and Marysarah Quinn; to my student Marilyn Toole for her end- less patience; and to all of my clients and students, who have given me much food for thought.

CONTENTS

"What you dislike in your superiors, avoid doing to your inferiors. What you dislike in your inferiors, avoid doing when working for your superiors. What you hate in those who are in front of you, do not do to those behind you. What you hate in those behind you, do not foist upon those in front of you. What you will not take from the right, do not give to the left. What you will not accept from the left, do not give to the right. This is called having the compass and measuring square of the Tao."

Confucius

FENG SHUI

STRATEGIES FOR BUSINESS SUCCESS

HOW TO USE THIS BOOK

Feng Shui Strategies for Business Success is primarily for people working in the business world. It not only addresses your personal path to success but also shows how to diagnose and positively affect the health of the company in which you are working.

Feng Shui Strategies for Business Success offers feng shui techniques traditionally applied to both military and commercial ventures. While written for the Westerner, it is on a par with similar manuals that have been in circulation among the power elite of China and Japan for many centuries. Although the equivalence of military and business strategies may not be readily apparent to the average Westerner, it is quite obvious to the Chinese, whose war god, Kwan Ti, or Emperor Kwan, is also the patron of business, wealth, and literature.

There is a famous image of Kwan Ti displayed prominently in many Chinese places of business. He stands in a green coat, red faced, in an attitude of fiery determination, making a gesture with his left hand symbolizing order, and grasping a lance in his right hand in a gesture symbolizing readiness to take action. Kwan Ti is the genius of tactical method. It is in Kwan Ti's spirit that this book is written.

The book is conceived as a logically organized system of easily accessible techniques that will give you, the reader, a unique advantage in your quest for success. It is intended to be dynamic and interactive. The best way to demonstrate this is to take a prototypical person, whom I shall call Sarah, through the process of using this book.

Sarah is an up-and-coming art director in an advertising firm. She is enthusi-astically dedicated to her goal of success within the company and wants to see the company prosper. Sarah's aim is to be promoted to a more prominent position, earn a larger salary, and have greater influence on the company's policies.

The company is relatively new. Since its inception it has faced serious com-petition in winning new clients and accounts. Recently the company suffered a major setback and, as a result, has been downsizing and reorganizing its staff.

Concerned about these developments and looking for ways she can improve conditions, Sarah reads *Feng Shui Strategies for Business Success*. In Part One she finds useful information regarding her personal aptitudes, her relationship with her boss, and her future prospects; in Part Two she finds information that helps her gauge the health of the company as it is affected by its physical surroundings, as well as the suitability of her office to her goals. Sarah also learns to recognize and use the elements of her physical surroundings to enhance her personal effective-ness in the company and discovers various ways to adjust and intensify the chi of her office so that it fully supports her and her professional goals.

Sarah's date of birth is September 30th, 1965, and she finds, by reading Chap-ters 2 and 3, that her year, month, and tendency stars are 7 Metal, 2 Earth, and 1 Water. Looking up the combination 7-2-1 in Chapter 3, Sarah reads:

> *You are highly sensitive, questioning, and resourceful. An astute conversational-*
> *ist and listener, you weigh sides of an issue carefully and take a long time to make*
> *up your mind; you do not trust easily. Your decisions and insights can surprise*
> *others. You love to be entertained and thrive where you work among supportive*
> *and enthusiastic people. But where others are unsupportive and out of harmony*
> *with you, you tend to lose interest in the projects at hand. Be that as it may, you*
> *always succeed by shrewd planning and perseverance. You have excellent social*
> *skills and artistic taste.*

Reassured that communication is her forte, Sarah wants to find out something about her relationship with her boss, Louise. Born in 1944, Louise has 4 Wood as her birth star. Looking up the combination of Louise's birth star with her own in Chapter 5, Sarah reads:

Because 4 Wood Star and 7 Metal Star are in conflict, your relationship could be tricky. Both of you are good communicators, and are sociable and accommodating, but 4 Wood acts out of emotional sensitivity, while 7 Metal is calculating and shrewd. Eventually, 4 Wood could question the sincerity of 7 Metal, and 7 Metal could question the motives of 4 Wood. You can be productive together when you share a common goal.

Forewarned of possible misunderstandings with her boss, Sarah wants to know whether her astrological forecast for the coming year favors her hopes of being promoted, and if it does which months will be appropriate for her to make her moves. Using the reference table in Chapter 6, she finds her yearly forecast. It reads:

Know who your friends are. You could be taken by surprise.

Favorable or unfavorable matters heretofore kept secret from you will come to light. Your secrets could become public knowledge as well. If your past business and financial dealings have been questionable, you could be exposed and have to suffer the consequences. . . . On the other hand, you could make surprisingly rapid progress, win the support of your colleagues and superiors, be promoted, or receive a surprise bonus, or if you are an artist, writer, or scientist, you may gain public recognition. Documents, signatures, meetings, and partings of the way count significantly in this period. You will receive the help and support of well-meaning colleagues and superiors when you need them.

Forewarned of risk and reassured of opportunity, Sarah reads through her twelve monthly forecasts and plans her best times to make her strategic moves. These forecasts, in a nutshell, are as follows:

For the period beginning

- Feb. 4   Although others favor you, you will not be able to advance your aims.
- Mar. 5   You will meet success through collaborating with a friend.
- Apr. 5   A superior will favor you.

- May 5 Wait and accept your limitations.
- June 6 To advance now will be easy and rewarding.
- July 7 You will be in a precarious position; pay attention to details.
- Aug. 7 A favorable period for business dealings and profits.
- Sept. 7 A pivotal month. Older projects will culminate while new plans for the future are being made.
- Oct. 8 An even period. Expect only minor gains and little recognition.
- Nov. 7 Although progress will be slow, your colleagues will be helpful.
- Dec. 7 Working in harmony with others will produce desired results.
- Jan. 5 You will receive the respect and support of your colleagues.

Next Sarah decides to arrange her office so that it fully supports her and promotes her aims. As she reads through Part Two, Sarah finds ideas that she can put to use easily.

Looking at the tables in Chapter 8, Sarah is pleased to find that the combination of her birth star, 7 Metal, and the Earth element of the northeast-facing door of her office are in perfect harmony. She is delighted also to find that her door fortune reads:

You will benefit through a partner. The key to your success here is cooperation. You will be promoted for your accomplishments.

Working with Chapter 8, Sarah detects a "tiger's head," a form of sha, or negative chi, through her office window. By using her compass Sarah determines that her office window looks to the southwest. Referring to the effects of sha, as determined by the compass direction from which it comes, Sarah learns that the tiger's head seen through the southwest-facing window of her office is injurious to her work. She also learns that she merely has to place a metal object of her choice on the windowsill to neutralize the undesirable effect of the tiger's head.

Next, while reading Chapters 9 and 10, Sarah examines her office for trouble spots. Finding nothing problematic, she turns to the instructions in Chapter 10 for enhancing the money and power points in her office for increased prosperity and luck, and she decides to use the beautiful talismans in Appendix II, which she cuts out and frames.

Finally, through reading the remaining chapters in Part Two, Sarah arrives at a full understanding of how to arrange her office in all its details. She places her desk, equipment, and other furniture in the most strategically advantageous positions and uses her lucky colors, found in Chapter 4, to decorate the room.

Having worked with Parts One and Two of the book, Sarah is as delighted with the new arrangement of her office as she is encouraged about her prospects for success, and she decides to try her hand at the special divination method in Appendix I. She finds it easy to use and understand, and discovers what a marvelously effective tool for strategic planning this method is; its unerring predictions are borne out time and time again. Sarah's story exemplifies the many possibilities for using *Feng Shui Strategies for Business Success*.

I envision this book as a precision instrument, a sort of navigational tool, that can be worked with in as many ways as there are individuals with unique professional aims. Because you will need to create a list of personal data in order to use the material in this book, I have provided the following framework for your Personal Data List which you need to fill out as you read the upcoming chapters.

To enjoy the full benefit of this book, read it chapter by chapter. Take your time to absorb the material. Once you understand it you will be able to work with it in a creative and powerful way.

PERSONAL DATA

1. The season in which you were born and its corresponding element. _____
_____

2. The yin or yang quality of the season in which you were born. _____

3. The element, or elements, corresponding to the business you are in. _____
_____

4. Your birth star and its element. _____

5. The yin or yang quality of your birth star. _____

6. The compass direction that corresponds to your birth star. _____

7. Compass directions in harmony with your birth star. _____
_____

8. The colors that correspond to your birth star. _____

9. The birth stars of your significant others. _____
_____

10. Your month star and its element. _____

11. The yin or yang quality of your month star. _____

12. The month stars of your significant others. _____
_____

13. Your tendency star and its element. _____

14. The yin or yang quality of your tendency star. _____

15. The tendency stars of your significant others. _____

16. Your predominant element. _____

17. Your predominant yin or yang quality. _____

18. Your lucky stars, with their corresponding directions in space, colors,
shapes, patterns, and images. _____
_____
_____

part one

THE ELEMENTS OF
YOUR CAREER

chapter 1

CHI, TIME, AND SPACE

In the West feng shui is generally called the art of placement. However, as traditionally used in Chinese and Japanese military and business strategies, feng shui is also an art of timing. Time is inextricably tied to space; time moves through space; there is no time without space.

Timing is the essence of strategy. Successful strategy involves discerning patterns and rhythms of change, and seizing the right moment for action. Feng shui is a study of the patterns of chi that enables one to manifest optimum conditions in one's environment.

Time implies change. In Chinese philosophy the principle of change is called chi. Chi moves in space. Time moves in space. Chi is cyclical. Change is cyclical. Cyclical changes are seen most readily in the seasons and the times of day.

Chi expresses its cyclical nature through two alternating phases, called *yin* and *yang*. Think of yin and yang as minus and plus, night and day, winter and summer, north and south, down and up.

In Chinese philosophy the cycle of chi is inseparably linked with the concepts of the Tao, the Tai Chi, or Great Ultimate, and the five elements: Water, Wood, Fire, Earth, and Metal.

Following Chinese philosophy, knowledge of the Tao and the Great Ultimate is central to the art of strategy. Lao Tzu alluded to this, saying, "Thirty spokes unite about one nave; but it is on that empty space that the use of the wheel depends." The Great Ultimate is calm and clear in the midst of change. When you truly center yourself, you are at one with the Great Ultimate. Acting in accord with the Great Ultimate, you are in accord with the Tao; and being in accord with the Tao, you have all the elements and processes of creation available to you. As Lao Tzu said, "Tao is the storehouse of all things," and "Tao produces all things."

THE TAO

Tao literally means "the way." It is that which is common to everything in the universe. Tao is absolute reality, the true meaning of which is beyond words. It is the essence of your very being. Lao Tzu says of Tao,

> *There was something undefined yet complete before heaven and earth.*
> *Still and formless, it stands alone and undergoes no change.*
> *It reaches everywhere and is inexhaustible. It may be regarded as*
> *the mother of the universe. I do not know its name. I call it Tao.*
> *Making an effort further to name it, I call it the Great. Great, it goes far.*
> *Having gone far, it returns to the point of origin. Therefore the Tao is great.*

THE TAI CHI, OR THE GREAT ULTIMATE

It is said that Tao produced the One. What is meant by the One is the Tai Chi, or Great Ultimate. The Great Ultimate and Tao are essentially one thing seen two ways. Tao implies absolute reality; the Great Ultimate implies relativity. Chuang Tzu calls the Great Ultimate "the pivot of the Tao." The pivot implies turning; turning implies opposites. Opposites are relative to each other. The Great Ultimate, therefore, is the ground of relativity. In terms of personal experience the Great Ultimate represents the ability to perceive differences and similarities and to establish relative values. Essentially, the Great Ultimate denotes the faculty of perception itself. If the Tao is the essence of your being, the Great Ultimate is your *awareness* of being.

CHI

As Tao produced the Tai Chi, it also produced chi. The Tai Chi and chi are simultaneous expressions of Tao. When it is motionless it is called the Tai Chi. When it moves it is called chi. Like the axle of a wheel, the Tai Chi is the core essence of chi.

Cyclical change is the effect of chi. Everything that exists in the universe is governed by chi. Everything that comes into existence evolves through cyclical change. Everything evolves through chi.

Chi also means spirit, or life force. It is the breath of nature. In terms of personal experience chi is your vital energy. When your chi is strong, your health is good. To cultivate your chi means to live a long and healthy life.

YIN AND YANG

Just as chi is cyclical, the course of chi is round. Being round chi rises and falls. *Yin* and *yang* are the names of the falling and rising phases of the cycle of chi. Yin falls. Yang rises. Yin and yang are opposite and complementary expressions of chi.

In the cycle of the seasons, autumn and winter are yin, spring and summer are yang. In the cycle of the day, the period of noon to midnight is yin, and the period of midnight to noon is yang. In the cycle of the moon, the period extending from full moon to new moon is yin, and the period extending from new moon to full moon is yang. In the cycle of your breathing, exhalation is yin and inhalation is yang. Yang expands, yin contracts. Yang is hard, yin is soft. Yang initiates, yin completes. Yang focuses, yin diffuses.

All people have both yin and yang qualities in their personalities. In some people the yin quality may be more pronounced, while in others the yang may be dominant. The yin personality most characteristically tends to be reflective, or introverted, and better suited to working quietly behind the scenes, whereas the yang personality most characteristically tends to be active, or extroverted, and better suited to working actively out in the world. You will be able to ascertain the balance of the yin and yang qualities of your personality after you read the next few chapters.

THE FIVE ELEMENTS AND YOUR SEASON OF BIRTH

The five elements are expressions of the yin and yang phases of chi. They are like moods. Their descriptive names are Water, Wood, Fire, Earth, and Metal. The nature of each of the five elements, and their correspondences to seasons and times of day, are as follows:

- Water: freezing and dissolving, or flowing; winter and night
- Wood: rising and flourishing; spring and morning
- Fire: expanding and lively; summer and noon
- Earth: balancing and gathering; late summer, the time of harvesting, and the afternoon
- Metal: containing and restricting; autumn and evening

Figure 1 shows how the five elements relate to the yin and yang phases of the cycle of chi. It also shows the correspondences of the five elements to the changing seasons and the times of day.

(fig. 1)

In addition to the seasons and times of day, the five elements have correspondences to personality characteristics, shapes, colors, directions in space, and businesses and occupations. As you read the descriptions of the five elements, please note the following:

- While your personality will display characteristics of your season of birth, don't assume that the element of the season in which you were born is the most pronounced element in your personality. Note on your Personal Data List the element of your birth season. After you have read through the first three chapters of this book, you will be able to determine which of the five elements is most pronounced in your personality.
- Some of the businesses listed here have correspondences with more than one element. For example, you will find that the entertainment industry has affinities with three elements: Wood, Fire, and Metal. As you read, note on your Personal Data List the element or elements corresponding to the business you are in. In Part Two I'll show you what to do with it all. Now let's look at each element in detail.

WATER

Water freezes and melts. Located between contracting Metal and expanding Wood, as seen in figure 1, Water denotes transition, and as such it corresponds to travel, commerce, sex, dreams, sleep, death, and birth. Because Water is cool and clear, it corresponds to reflection and deep concentration. Running deep underground, Water corresponds to secrecy. Rushing along rapids and over waterfalls, Water also corresponds to passions and desires.

YOUR SEASON OF BIRTH

If you were born in the winter, the season of the element Water, a yin season that in the Chinese calendar falls between November 7th and February 4th, your personality may display such characteristics as changeableness, insecurity, secrecy, and intense emotionality. On the other hand, you could be phlegmatic or even cold and sluggish. To keep your Water nature healthy and flowing, cultivate your innate abilities to reflect calmly, to see both sides of an argument, and to be adaptable while pursuing the object of your desire.

SHAPE, COLORS, AND DIRECTION IN SPACE

The shape of Water is asymmetrical and flowing. Buildings with undulating curves correspond to Water. The colors of Water are black and the deepest of blues. The compass direction is north.

BUSINESSES AND APTITUDES

Businesses corresponding to Water involve all forms of transit, transportation, shipping, trucking, import-export, and financial exchanges, as well as sales, printing, dyeing, pharmaceuticals, refrigeration, air-conditioning, sprinkling systems, plumbing, public utilities, laundries, health spas, hospitals, hotels, restaurants, bars, breweries, wineries, dairies, fisheries, films, plastics, oil companies, paints and varnishes, all kinds of maintenance, and prosthetics.

If you find that Water is pronounced in your personality, you have aptitudes for occupations that involve deep thought and reflection. You could be a scientist, statistical researcher, systems analyst, detective, investigator, salesperson, social worker, psychotherapist, pharmacist, medical researcher, nurse, or medical technician, especially in anesthesiology.

WOOD

Wood rises and flourishes. It springs up and branches out, putting forth leaves, flowers, fruits, and seeds. Located between Water and Fire, as seen in figure 1, Wood denotes growth. It draws nourishment from the cold water deep underground and reaches up to the sun. As such, Wood corresponds to aspirations, plans, developments, strategies, and decisions. Because Wood bends and is resilient, it corresponds to bows and arrows, bridges and airplanes. Because Wood snaps when pressured too much, it corresponds to anger, shouting, and gunpowder. On a happier note, Wood corresponds to music.

YOUR SEASON OF BIRTH

If you were born in the spring, the season of the element Wood, a yang season that in the Chinese calendar falls between February 4th and May 5th, your personality may display such characteristics as youthfulness, ambition, optimism, aspiration, high spirits, impulsiveness, impatience, single-mindedness, and stubbornness. It is your way to rise rapidly and against all odds. Cultivate your imaginative and creative abilities as well as your romantic and spiritual qualities to keep your Wood nature healthy and resilient.

SHAPE, COLORS, AND DIRECTIONS IN SPACE

The shape of Wood is rectangular. High-rise buildings with flat roofs correspond to Wood. The colors of Wood are all the shades of green and the lighter shades of blue. The compass directions are east and southeast.

BUSINESSES AND APTITUDES

Businesses corresponding to Wood involve designing, planning, and disseminating information. They include all technical fields, computer engineering, architectural design and decorating, graphics, advertising, communications, public relations, news and all information media, postal and delivery services, the travel industry, airlines, railroads, the automobile industry, taxi and limousine services, elevators, telephones, telephone answering services, doorbell and alarm systems, munitions, the radio and television industries, the music and recording industries, the movie industry, cinematography, camera manufacturing, photography, lighting and light fixtures, textiles, paper and lumber companies, furniture stores and manufacturing, building materials, construction companies, contracting, printing, sign making, translation services, and all sports-related industries.

If you find that Wood is pronounced in your personality, you have aptitudes for occupations in computer programming and engineering, computer program architecture, electrical engineering, radio, television, public relations, teaching, lecturing, writing, filming, editing, printing, designing, drafting, painting, music, architectural and interior design, furniture design, fashion design, and the building trades. You could also be an engineer, surgeon, journalist, photographer, court reporter, office worker, bookkeeper, auditor, secretary, telephone operator, office manager, messenger, agent, attorney, transportation worker, salesperson, post office employee, vendor, or athlete.

FIRE

Fire rises and inspirits. Like the sun extending its rays over the world, Fire denotes the exercise of authority and corresponds to systems of government and management. Because it glows and radiates, Fire corresponds to public appearances and beauty. Because Fire is warm, it corresponds to all that inspires happiness. Fire is entirely dependent on a host in order to exist. Fire clings. As such it corresponds to dependence and compliance, and our common need for a harmonious society. Fire is elusive. It vanishes into thin air, so it corresponds to all that is glamorous. Fire, because it is hot, also corresponds to open dialogues, public debates, contests, and wars.

YOUR SEASON OF BIRTH

If you were born in the summer, the season of the element Fire, a yang season that in the Chinese calendar falls between May 5th and August 7th, your personality may display such characteristics as zealousness, passion, ardor, and love of amusement. Cultivate your abilities to be kindhearted, compassionate, generous, and sociable to keep your Fire nature healthy and high-spirited.

SHAPE, COLORS, AND DIRECTION IN SPACE

The shape of Fire is sharp and pointed. Buildings with roofs resembling an inverted V, or with spires or steeples, correspond to Fire. The colors of Fire include all the purples, pinks, roses, and reds. The compass direction is south.

BUSINESSES AND APTITUDES

Organizations and businesses corresponding to Fire include government organizations; the entertainment field in general, including theater, television, radio, and cinema; speculation, as in commodities and stock brokerage; department stores; toys; the fashion industry; cosmetics; beauty salons; art galleries; publishing companies; schools; cooking utensil manufacture; stoves and heating systems; fire departments; optics and optometry; electricity and electrical appliances; interior decorating; landscaping; and garden design.

If you find that Fire is pronounced in your personality, you have aptitudes for such occupations as diplomat, politician, lawyer, judge, medical doctor, minister, actor, teacher, public personality, advertiser, publicist, reporter, journalist, publisher, editor, book dealer, writer, artist, stock and commodities broker, fashion designer, cosmetician, beautician, jeweler, optometrist, electrician, electrical engineer, interior decorator, garden designer, or medical technician, especially in the area of radiology.

EARTH

Earth supports life. Located between the expansive Fire and the contracting Metal, as seen in figure 1, Earth denotes transition. Earth gathers and settles. Earth collects all that is dead and transforms it to living matter. As such Earth denotes usefulness and service. Like mountains that act as natural boundaries and contain precious minerals, Earth denotes barriers, storage units, and banks.

YOUR SEASON OF BIRTH

Earth has no one season of its own; all seasons belong to it. However Earth is strongest at the end of summer. If you were born in late summer, a yin season that in the Chinese calendar falls between July 23rd and August 7th, your personality may display, in addition to the warmth and high energy of Fire, such characteristics as reliability, determination, practicality, gentleness, and thoughtfulness. Cultivate your creative and inventive abilities to keep your Earth nature healthy and productive.

SHAPE, COLORS, AND DIRECTIONS IN SPACE

The shape of Earth is broad, flat, and square. Buildings that are low, broad, and square correspond to Earth. The colors of Earth are all the earth tones, beige, browns, oranges, and yellows. The compass directions are southwest and northeast. In addition to these, Earth is always in the middle of any given space.

BUSINESSES AND APTITUDES

Organizations corresponding to Earth provide needed services and staples. They include the entire food industry—farming, food processing, packaging, bakeries, supermarkets, grocers, caterers, candy and ice cream shops—shoe and clothing manufacturers and stores, home furnishings, real estate, financial services, banks, savings and loan institutions, collection agencies, insurance companies, investment brokerage, antiques, fine arts dealers, watchmakers, precision instrument and fine tool manufacturing, health services, clinics, hospitals, health food companies and stores, hotels, motels, beds and mattresses, storage and warehouse companies, security, and philanthropic organizations.

If you find that Earth is pronounced in your personality, you have aptitudes for such occupations as banker, bank teller, financial institution employee, broker, treasurer, accountant, dealer in valuable commodities and furnishings, real estate broker, executive, director, manager, secretary, judge, land developer, carpenter, builder, dealer in leather goods, dealer in clocks and watches, watchmaker, troubleshooter, hairdresser, osteopath, pediatrician, general practitioner, nurse, hospital worker, dietitian, dentist, physical education trainer, waiter, veterinarian, shopkeeper, food, shoes, and clothes salesperson, antiques dealer, gardener, serviceperson, or caretaker.

METAL

Metal is a crystalline substance that grows out of Earth. It possesses such qualities as ductility, malleability, and conductivity. Metal can be drawn into wires, bent into any shape, and used to conduct heat, electricity, light, and sound. Metal is versatile. It can be both flexible and rigid. It is used in thousands of ways. In Chinese philosophy Metal is associated with heaven; the creative principle; the highest levels of status, power, and culture; the military; law; wealth; nobility; bravery; leadership; high-spiritedness; and the ability to communicate.

YOUR SEASON OF BIRTH

If you were born in the autumn, the season of Metal, a yin season that in the Chinese calendar falls between August 7th and November 7th, your personality may display such characteristics as orderliness, firmness, decisiveness, organizational and leadership abilities, the ability to control, practicality, creativity, courage, daring, and discipline. Cultivate your abilities to set healthy boundaries and to communicate to keep your Metal nature in balance.

SHAPES, COLORS, AND DIRECTIONS IN SPACE

The shapes of Metal are round and oval. Buildings that have arched roofs, domes, or cupolas correspond to Metal. The colors of Metal are white, silver, and gray. The compass directions are west and northwest.

BUSINESSES AND APTITUDES

Organizations corresponding to Metal involve the use of computers, high-tech instruments, and communications systems and devices. Organizations and businesses corresponding to Metal include government and military services, the legal profession, the computer industry, public relations, communications systems, entertainment, restaurants and cabarets, savings and loan institutions, stock and bond brokerage houses, dental clinics, machine manufacturing, construction equipment, electrical wiring, and companies dealing in perfumes, jewelry, mirrors, bottles and containers, plastics, cutlery and cooking utensils, automobiles, and sports equipment.

If you find that Metal is pronounced in your personality, you have aptitudes for such occupations as computer technician, teacher, lawyer, government or military official, manager, director, chairperson, banker, broker, salesperson, public relations agent, dentist, or jeweler.

THE THREE CYCLES

In addition to their correspondences, the five elements have three basic ways, or cycles, of interacting with one another: the cycle of generation, the cycle of destruction, and the cycle of mitigation. Let's examine the cycles of generation and destruction first. The interactions of the elements can be seen in figure 2.

THE CYCLE OF GENERATION	THE CYCLE OF DESTRUCTION
Water generates (or nourishes) Wood	Water destroys (or extinguishes) Fire
Wood generates (or feeds) Fire	Fire destroys (or melts) Metal
Fire generates (or produces) Earth	Metal destroys (or cuts) Wood
Earth generates (or produces) Metal	Wood destroys (or breaks) Earth
Metal generates (or supports) Water	Earth destroys (or stops) Water

(*fig. 2*)

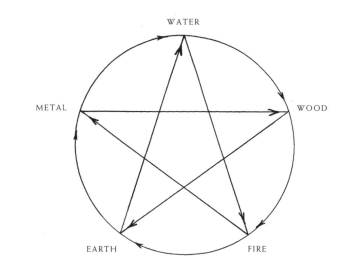

Following the arrows in figure 2, the elements going clockwise around the circle constitute the cycle of generation, while the arrows within the star formation show the cycle of destruction. Note how the order of destruction is formed by skipping an element on the circle. For example, Water generates Wood, Wood generates Fire, and Water destroys Fire. Note also how the skipped element becomes the mitigating element in the destructive relationship of the two elements on either side of it. For example, in the sequence Water, Wood, and Fire, Wood mitigates, or neutralizes, the destructive relationship of Water and Fire. Here is the complete cycle of mitigation:

THE CYCLE OF MITIGATION
Water mitigates the conflict of Metal and Wood
Wood mitigates the conflict of Water and Fire
Fire mitigates the conflict of Wood and Earth
Earth mitigates the conflict of Fire and Metal
Metal mitigates the conflict of Earth and Water

EXERCISE

On your Personal Data List:

- Write down the season in which you were born and its element.
- Write down the yin or yang quality of the season in which you were born.
- Write down the element, or elements, corresponding to the business you are in.

Please wait until you have read through Chapters 2 and 3 to determine the elements corresponding to your personal aptitudes.

chapter 2

THE NINE STARS: YOUR BASIC PERSONALITY

Nine star astrology, the oldest and simplest form of Chinese astrology, originated in the twenty-ninth century B.C. from divination methods employed by the emperor Fu Hsi. Traditionally associated with the North Star, the seven stars of the Big Dipper, and the star Wega, the nine stars are in fact yin and yang expressions of the five elements. The names given to the nine stars are 1 Water Star, 2 Earth Star, 3 Wood Star, 4 Wood Star, 5 Earth Star, 6 Metal Star, 7 Metal Star, 8 Earth Star, and 9 Fire Star.

Viewing the nine stars in their compass arrangement, called in Chinese the Lo Shu diagram, shown in figure 3, you can see them with their yin and yang correspondences as well as their corresponding directions in space.

(fig. 3)

LO SHU DIAGRAM

	SE	S	SW
	4 WOOD YIN	9 FIRE YANG	2 EARTH YIN
E	3 WOOD YANG	5 EARTH YIN/YANG	7 METAL YIN	W
	8 EARTH YANG	1 WATER YIN	6 METAL YANG
	NE	N	NW

Following the Lo Shu diagram, you will notice that 9 Fire Star and 1 Water Star are in opposite positions. 1 Water Star is called the Great Yin; 9 Fire Star is called the Great Yang. You also will notice that 2 Earth Star, which is yin, and 8 Earth Star, which is yang, are in opposite positions, while 5 Earth Star, in the middle of the diagram, is both yin and yang at once. Finally, 3 Wood Star, which is yang, is opposite 7 Metal Star, which is yin, and 4 Wood Star, which is yin, is opposite 6 Metal Star, which is yang. So you see that the yin and yang qualities are always opposite each other in the Lo Shu diagram, and that they converge at 5 Earth Star in the middle.

Each of the nine stars has a characteristic image that evokes its essential meaning. Here is a table of the nine stars, with their yin and yang qualities, corresponding compass directions, and classical images:

THE NINE STARS

STAR AND ELEMENT	YIN/YANG QUALITY	COMPASS DIRECTION	IMAGE
1 Water Star	Yin	North	Moon
2 Earth Star	Yin	Southwest	Valley
3 Wood Star	Yang	East	Thunder
4 Wood Star	Yin	Southeast	Wind
5 Earth Star	Yin/Yang	Middle	Pivot
6 Metal Star	Yang	Northwest	Sky
7 Metal Star	Yin	West	Lake
8 Earth Star	Yang	Northeast	Mountain
9 Fire Star	Yang	South	Sun

In nine star astrology, because every year and month is ruled by a different star/element, the stars of the year and month you were born describe your personality. Your stars also indicate the best colors for you to use, as well as the best directions in space for the alignment of your key furniture, such as your desk and chair. Let's look first at what the star of your year of birth has to say.

YOUR BIRTH STAR

The following table contains birth stars for each year from 1905 through 2013. Nine star astrology is based on the Chinese solar calendar, which begins on February 4th, not January 1st. This means that if you were born between January 1st and February 4th, you will use the year before your Western year of birth to find your birth star. For example, if you were born on January 20th, 1961, you would look up your birth star under 1960. Also note that males and females born in the same year generally have different stars.

BIRTH STARS

YEAR OF BIRTH	MALE STAR	FEMALE STAR
1905	5 Earth	1 Water
1906	4 Wood	2 Earth
1907	3 Wood	3 Wood
1908	2 Earth	4 Wood
1909	1 Water	5 Earth
1910	9 Fire	6 Metal
1911	8 Earth	7 Metal
1912	7 Metal	8 Earth
1913	6 Metal	9 Fire
1914	5 Earth	1 Water
1915	4 Wood	2 Earth
1916	3 Wood	3 Wood
1917	2 Earth	4 Wood
1918	1 Water	5 Earth
1919	9 Fire	6 Metal
1920	8 Earth	7 Metal
1921	7 Metal	8 Earth
1922	6 Metal	9 Fire
1923	5 Earth	1 Water
1924	4 Wood	2 Earth
1925	3 Wood	3 Wood
1926	2 Earth	4 Wood

Year of Birth	Male Star	Female Star
1927	1 Water	5 Earth
1928	9 Fire	6 Metal
1929	8 Earth	7 Metal
1930	7 Metal	8 Earth
1931	6 Metal	9 Fire
1932	5 Earth	1 Water
1933	4 Wood	2 Earth
1934	3 Wood	3 Wood
1935	2 Earth	4 Wood
1936	1 Water	5 Earth
1937	9 Fire	6 Metal
1938	8 Earth	7 Metal
1939	7 Metal	8 Earth
1940	6 Metal	9 Fire
1941	5 Earth	1 Water
1942	4 Wood	2 Earth
1943	3 Wood	3 Wood
1944	2 Earth	4 Wood
1945	1 Water	5 Earth
1946	9 Fire	6 Metal
1947	8 Earth	7 Metal
1948	7 Metal	8 Earth
1949	6 Metal	9 Fire
1950	5 Earth	1 Water
1951	4 Wood	2 Earth
1952	3 Wood	3 Wood
1953	2 Earth	4 Wood
1954	1 Water	5 Earth
1955	9 Fire	6 Metal
1956	8 Earth	7 Metal
1957	7 Metal	8 Earth
1958	6 Metal	9 Fire
1959	5 Earth	1 Water
1960	4 Wood	2 Earth

YEAR OF BIRTH	MALE STAR	FEMALE STAR
1961	3 Wood	3 Wood
1962	2 Earth	4 Wood
1963	1 Water	5 Earth
1964	9 Fire	6 Metal
1965	8 Earth	7 Metal
1966	7 Metal	8 Earth
1967	6 Metal	9 Fire
1968	5 Earth	1 Water
1969	4 Wood	2 Earth
1970	3 Wood	3 Wood
1971	2 Earth	4 Wood
1972	1 Water	5 Earth
1973	9 Fire	6 Metal
1974	8 Earth	7 Metal
1975	7 Metal	8 Earth
1976	6 Metal	9 Fire
1977	5 Earth	1 Water
1978	4 Wood	2 Earth
1979	3 Wood	3 Wood
1980	2 Earth	4 Wood
1981	1 Water	5 Earth
1982	9 Fire	6 Metal
1983	8 Earth	7 Metal
1984	7 Metal	8 Earth
1985	6 Metal	9 Fire
1986	5 Earth	1 Water
1987	4 Wood	2 Earth
1988	3 Wood	3 Wood
1989	2 Earth	4 Wood
1990	1 Water	5 Earth
1991	9 Fire	6 Metal
1992	8 Earth	7 Metal
1993	7 Metal	8 Earth
1994	6 Metal	9 Fire
1995	5 Earth	1 Water

YEAR OF BIRTH	MALE STAR	FEMALE STAR
1996	4 Wood	2 Earth
1997	3 Wood	3 Wood
1998	2 Earth	4 Wood
1999	1 Water	5 Earth
2000	9 Fire	6 Metal
2001	8 Earth	7 Metal
2002	7 Metal	8 Earth
2003	6 Metal	9 Fire
2004	5 Earth	1 Water
2005	4 Wood	2 Earth
2006	3 Wood	3 Wood
2007	2 Earth	4 Wood
2008	1 Water	5 Earth
2009	9 Fire	6 Metal
2010	8 Earth	7 Metal
2011	7 Metal	8 Earth
2012	6 Metal	9 Fire
2013	5 Earth	1 Water

Each of the nine stars describes a basic personality. Following the order of generation of the elements, the stars are grouped as follows: 1 Water Star; 3 and 4 Wood Stars; 9 Fire Star; 2, 5, and 8 Earth Stars; 6 and 7 Metal Stars. Where two or three stars are listed under one element, a general personality description of the element precedes the personality descriptions of its related stars. You will find included with the description of each star a list of favorable directions in space.

1 WATER STAR (YIN)

Like the moon, your mind is constantly changing and fluctuating. You are inwardly restless even though outwardly calm. Although you may appear quiet and mild, you can be stubborn, ambitious, and competitive, and will try to force others to do your bidding. You have the ability to be secretive and to read minds. Try to avoid the temptation to manipulate others through flattery and pretense.

The chi of 1 Water Star is most intense if you were born in the autumn or winter, tends to be mild if you were born in the spring, and is most subtle if you were born in the summer or at the end of summer.

YOUR FINANCIAL OUTLOOK

You are basically thrifty and conservative with money. You prefer not to take big risks but build up your fortunes slowly and steadily. You would do well to invest in real estate, securities, and valuable insurance policies.

YOUR HEALTH

The positive mental states of Water are adaptability, reflection, intelligence, willpower, and healthy ambition. The negative mental states of Water are fear, anxiety, and depression. The parts of the body associated with Water are the adrenals, kidneys, bladder, sexual organs, nerves, brain, lymph, blood, bone marrow, bones, teeth, inner ear, the hair on your head, and the senses of hearing and taste. Symptoms in any of these parts of the body, including chronic anxiety, depression, other emotional and mental disorders, and poor circulation, hemorrhoids, hardening of the arteries, and senility, are indications of unbalanced Water.

Maintaining a balanced diet, exercising, and cultivating inner peace and steady concentration are your keys to good health. Excessive worry, laziness, overeating, undereating, drinking, giving in to your sweet tooth, and addiction to medicines can result in poor health. Some foods traditionally used to nourish Water functioning are azuki beans, kidney beans, buckwheat, seaweed, saltwater fish, and pork. The taste of salt stimulates Water functioning.

YOUR DIRECTIONS AND COLORS

The direction in space for 1 Water Star is north. Other harmonious directions are east, southeast, west, and northwest. Colors are black, the deepest blues, and white.

THE WOOD PERSONALITY

The two Wood stars are 3 Wood Star and 4 Wood Star. If you were born under either of them, you are naturally optimistic, enthusiastic, energetic, creative, aspiring, expansive, progressive, trustworthy, ethical, and loyal. You have natural aptitudes for planning and designing. The chi of 3 and 4 Wood Stars is strongest if you were born in the winter or spring, tends to be mild if you were born in the summer, and is most subtle if you were born at the end of summer or in the autumn.

The positive mental states of Wood are kindness, adventurousness, curiosity, and the ability to make decisions. The negative mental states of Wood are anger and confusion. The parts of the body associated with Wood are the liver, gallbladder, muscles, tendons, connective tissue, joints, hands and feet, eyes, and the senses of sight and touch. Symptoms in any of these parts of the body, or hypertension caused by stress, or the habitual tendency to complain and become irritable, angry, and abusive are indications of unbalanced Wood. Some foods traditionally used to nourish Wood are barley, oats, wheat, cauliflower, green vegetables, sprouts, bamboo shoots, onions, leeks, garlic, citrus fruits, plums, peaches, rice vinegar, and poultry. The taste of sour stimulates Wood functioning.

Let's look now at each Wood star individually.

3 WOOD STAR (YANG)

Like thunder, you are full of surprises. You are naturally kindhearted, gentle, tender, cheerful, and courageous. Acting on the spur of the moment, as you tend to do, can work both for and against you. If you do not cultivate flexibility, you can snap under pressure. To your chagrin, your anger can frighten others. You need to cultivate patience to see long-range plans come to fruition.

YOUR FINANCIAL OUTLOOK

You can go to extremes in financial gains and losses, making it difficult to build up your fortunes. Your love of action may attract you to playing the stock and commodities markets, which can take you on a roller-coaster ride if you are not careful. You would do well to control your spending impulses.

YOUR HEALTH

Your key to good health is to stay flexible and agile in body and mind. You need to cultivate the ability to release all undue stress from your life; you are prone to liver and gallbladder problems as well as mental and nervous breakdowns. You would be wise to avoid most stimulants and drugs. You need to be able to balance vigorous activity with relaxation. You will benefit from spending periods of time in nature, where you can get fresh air and sunlight.

YOUR DIRECTIONS AND COLORS

The direction in space for 3 Wood Star is east. Other harmonious directions are north, southeast, and south. Colors are the lighter shades of green and blue.

4 WOOD STAR (YIN)

Like the wind, your mind flows. You are naturally gentle. However, you can become extremely restless and, when under too much pressure, can become quite stormy. You may tend to have scattered interests and to overwork. You may also tend to worry about the future, become indecisive and confused, and procrastinate over decisions while you change your mind repeatedly. Indecision causes you to miss opportunities. It is generally better for you to work for others than to have others work for you. Nonetheless, it is both interesting and easy for you to freelance with an occupation that offers you a variety of projects.

YOUR FINANCIAL OUTLOOK

You need to learn how to build up your finances. You can easily spend all you earn. Do not naively trust those who, resorting to shady practices, cause you financial losses. Your key to financial growth is diversity. You could do well by investing in stocks, bonds, and real estate.

YOUR HEALTH

Your key to good health is to balance work with recreation and relaxation. Overwork can result in a severe mental and nervous condition, as well as in weakening of the immune function, intestinal problems, respiratory troubles, back pains, and colds. You are also susceptible to liver and gallbladder complaints.

YOUR DIRECTIONS AND COLORS

The direction in space for 4 Wood Star is southeast. Other harmonious directions are north, east, and south. Colors are the deeper shades of green and rich blues.

9 FIRE STAR (YANG)

Like the sun, you shine and love to attract attention. Appearances are important to you. Having expensive tastes, you are inclined to live beyond your means. You are egotistical and capable of leading others. You are also quick-tempered and competitive, and can be severely critical of others. Even though you have a large circle of acquaintances, few can say they know you well. While you want to be loved and admired, your great need for privacy makes it difficult for others to understand your elusive and fiery nature. You are a gifted speaker and are artistically inclined. The chi of 9 Fire Star is strongest if you were born in the spring or summer, tends to be mild if you were born at the end of summer, and is most subtle if you were born in the autumn or winter.

YOUR FINANCIAL OUTLOOK

Because you can be unrealistic about money and spend all you make, it will be difficult for you to amass wealth. However, if you follow your hunches and take advantage of your opportunities while curbing your spending impulses, you can become quite wealthy. Your instinct for speculating could lead you to play the commodities and stock markets. Be careful!

YOUR HEALTH

The positive mental states of Fire are brightness, intuition, playfulness, cheerfulness, love, and compassion. The negative mental state of Fire is hysteria. The parts of the body associated with Fire are the heart, small intestine, "triple heater" (ruling the digestive process and ability to regulate body heat), the "heart constrictor" (ruling the heartbeat and circulation of the blood, as well as the emotions of joy and sorrow), blood vessels, ears, tongue, complexion, eyes, and the faculty of speech. Symptoms in any of these parts of the body, including hearing and speech impediments as well as tendencies toward mental illness and nervous disorders, are indications of unbalanced Fire.

Your key to good health is to balance your heart and to cultivate compassion. Emotional extremes can result in health problems. Some foods traditionally used to nourish Fire are corn, red pepper, large, leafy green vegetables, peanuts, shellfish, and lamb and mutton. Bitter tastes stimulate Fire functioning.

YOUR DIRECTIONS AND COLORS

The direction in space for 9 Fire Star is south. Other harmonious directions are east, southeast, southwest, and northeast. Colors are all the reds, pinks, roses, and purples.

THE EARTH PERSONALITY

The three Earth stars are 2 Earth Star, 5 Earth Star, and 8 Earth Star. If you were born under any of them, you are naturally conservative, practical, slow to decide, careful, and protective. You have natural aptitudes for working in such basic areas as food, real estate, medicine, clothing, and finance. The chi of 2, 5, and 8 Earth Stars is strongest if you were born in the summer or at the end of summer, tends to be mild if you were born in the autumn, and is most subtle if you were born in the winter or spring.

The positive mental states of Earth are trustworthiness, steadiness, sympathy, reliability, faithfulness, supportiveness, and moderation. The negative mental state of Earth is worry. The parts of the body associated with Earth are the stomach, spleen, pancreas, mouth, throat, flesh, and the nose as the organ of smell. Symptoms in any of these parts of the body, including impaired sense of smell and habitual tendencies to worry, to be confused, forgetful, unsettled, selfish, and/or greedy, are indications of unbalanced Earth. Some foods traditionally used to nourish Earth are millet, squash, carrots, beets, chickpeas, yams, taro, sweet potatoes, mushrooms, avocados, and beef. Sweet, agreeable tastes stimulate Earth functioning.

Let's look now at each Earth star individually.

2 EARTH STAR (YIN)

Like the valley, your mind is fertile and productive. You are receptive and caring, honest and tenacious. However, you tend to be insecure, and being unsure of your own decisions you may become dependent on someone else for support and guidance. This can work well or ill for you, depending upon whom you are depending on. You tend to be loyal and jealous. You learn quickly and enjoy helping others.

YOUR FINANCIAL OUTLOOK

You are not a great risk taker and prefer to save your money rather than speculate with it. However, you can benefit by investing in real estate, treasury bills, and municipal bonds.

YOUR HEALTH

Your key to good health is to pay attention to your diet and to exercise. Addiction to sweets, a sedentary lifestyle, and the tendency to worry can result in health problems affecting your digestive system and intestines. You are susceptible to stomach ulcers, diabetes, blood disorders, thyroid conditions, throat ailments, skin diseases, backache, problems of assimilation, torpidity, and obesity.

YOUR DIRECTIONS AND COLORS

The direction in space for 2 Earth Star is southwest. Other harmonious directions are west, northwest, northeast, and south. Colors are beige, all the browns, tans, oranges, yellows, and black.

5 EARTH STAR (YIN AND YANG)

Like a pivot, you see yourself as the center of your world; everything revolves around you. It is essential for you to define your boundaries and to take control of your circumstances in order to stay on top. You either rise or sink in life. You are strong willed and stubborn, and have the ability to become a leader and take on great responsibilities. You tend to resist pressure and are discontented in a subordinate position unless it offers you a real opportunity to rise to greater power.

Despite your gentle appearance you become unyielding, suspicious, and argumentative under stress. Beware of overestimating your abilities; you can make enemies.

YOUR FINANCIAL OUTLOOK

You are generally lucky with money and have the knack of amassing great wealth, because you are farsighted and frugal. Being conservative by nature, you can make money in real estate and in securities. However, all high-risk speculating and get-rich-quick schemes are sure ways for you to lose.

YOUR HEALTH

Your key to good health is not to overwork. You have abundant vital energy and resistance, and thrive on physical exercise. Neglecting your diet and overworking can lead to heart disease and circulatory problems, digestive problems, diabetes, weakened immune function, infectious diseases, and tumors.

YOUR DIRECTIONS AND COLORS

The direction in space for 5 Earth Star for men is southwest and for women is northeast. Other harmonious directions are northeast, south, southwest, west, and northwest. Colors are beige, all the yellows, browns, tans, and oranges.

8 EARTH STAR (YANG)

Like the mountain, you rise above the crowd and stand apart. You are strong willed, self-contained, and self-protective, and you do not like to cooperate with others unless it is to your ultimate advantage. You have a tendency to worry and be suspicious about other people's motives, and you can lose many precious opportunities if you let your doubts overrule you.

YOUR FINANCIAL OUTLOOK

You are generally fortunate with money. You have excellent abilities for financial planning and can build up a fortune by diversifying your investments. You tend to be secretive about your money and are provident for the future. You are attracted to real estate and other conservative investments.

YOUR HEALTH

Your key to good health is exercise. Sedentary habits will lead you to suffer from chronic illnesses. You need to watch your diet. You are prone to digestive, intestinal, and circulatory problems, as well as diabetes, ulcers, arthritis, general weakness, and hypochondria.

YOUR DIRECTIONS AND COLORS

The direction in space for 8 Earth Star is northeast. Other harmonious directions are southwest, west, northwest, and south. Colors are beige, all the browns, tans, oranges, yellows, and white.

THE METAL PERSONALITY

The two Metal stars are 6 Metal Star and 7 Metal Star. If you were born under one of them, you are a natural perfectionist. You set high standards and are idealistic. You have strong communication and social skills; are an excellent organizer, critic, and creative thinker; and have aptitudes for the financial industries. The chi of 6 and 7 Metal Stars is strongest if you were born at the end of summer or in the autumn, tends to be mild if you were born in the winter, and is most subtle if you were born in the spring or summer.

The positive mental states of Metal are self-confidence and self-discipline. The negative mental state of Metal is grief. The parts of the body associated with Metal are the lungs, large intestine, skin, body hair, and the nose as breathing apparatus. Symptoms in any of these parts of the body, and the habitual tendencies to grieve, to be rigidly controlling, and to refuse to communicate with others, are indications of unbalanced Metal. Some foods traditionally used to nourish Metal are rice, rye, soy, root vegetables, tea, wine, ginger, and freshwater fish. Pungent tastes stimulate Metal functioning.

Let's look now at each Metal star individually.

6 METAL STAR (YANG)

Like the sky, you aspire to rise above everything and everyone. You are generally straightforward and honest, even to the point of being blunt. Intelligent and quick-tempered as you are, it is difficult for you to tolerate the shortcomings and weaknesses of others. You tend to be autocratic and find those who criticize you or give you advice annoying; listening is not one of your strong points. You are ambitious and determined to be a winner. You are prone to excessive worry, and, in struggling to rise to the top, may make a few enemies. You tend to conceal your motives, and when conflict arises you can become ruthless. However, once you attain your objective you become protective of those under you. You make a good and demanding boss, setting high standards.

YOUR FINANCIAL OUTLOOK

In general the older you become, the more financially fortunate you become. Whatever difficulties you have in your earlier years should give way to greater and greater prosperity. Although frugal by nature, you like to think on a large scale. You could make a fortune in real estate and in the stock market.

YOUR HEALTH

Your key to good health is to stay in good spirits. Overwork, worry, and joyless-ness can lead to problems of the lungs and intestines. You are susceptible to heart ailments and nervous upsets as well.

YOUR DIRECTIONS AND COLORS

The direction in space for 6 Metal Star is northwest. Other harmonious directions are southwest, west, north, and northeast. Colors are white, silver, and gray.

7 METAL STAR (YIN)

Like the lake, you are reflective and playful. You are a gifted conversationalist and writer, and you have the ability to charm and influence others with your smooth manner and wit. You are naturally skillful with people. Try to avoid manipulating others through flattery and cunning. A keen observer of others, you are capable of criticizing people behind their backs while using their weaknesses to your advantage. Keeping double standards will spell your downfall in the long run. Notwithstanding, because you are sharp minded and detail oriented, you make a good critic and counselor, and are at your best in a good partnership. You need a socially active and friendly environment in order to feel secure and happy with your work.

YOUR FINANCIAL OUTLOOK

You are generally fortunate with money, earning as much as you want to spend. You see money as a means to an end, knowing thoroughly how to enjoy yourself. You are never without for long, and in later years you will tend to build up sufficient wealth to be comfortable. If you have a taste for gambling, you are sure to lose more than you make. Avoid high-risk speculating.

YOUR HEALTH

Your key to good health is moderation, hard as that may seem. Overindulgence can lead to digestive problems, intestinal troubles, and illnesses affecting the mouth, teeth, tongue, throat, and lungs. You are also susceptible to arthritis of the lower back, pelvic region, and hips; venereal diseases; and kidney problems.

YOUR DIRECTIONS AND COLORS

The direction in space for 7 Metal Star is west. Other harmonious directions are southwest, northwest, north, and northeast. Colors are white and the lighter hues of red, but not pink.

EXERCISE

On your Personal Data List:

- Write down your birth star and element (1 Water, 2 Earth, and so on).
- Write down the yin or yang quality of your birth star.
- Write down the compass direction that corresponds to your birth star.
- Write down the compass directions in harmony with your birth star.
- Write down the colors that correspond to your birth star.
- Write down the birth stars of your significant others.

THE
NINE
STARS

YOUR
BASIC
PERSONALITY

chapter 3

YOUR
TENDENCY STAR

Your tendency star is revealed by the combination of your birth star and the star of your month of birth. To find your month star, you first have to determine the Chinese solar month of your birth. There are twelve solar months in the Chinese solar calendar. These months have no names but are assigned numbers 1 through 12. The twelve Chinese months, with their equivalent Western dates, are as follows:

CHINESE SOLAR MONTHS

CHINESE MONTH	EQUIVALENT WESTERN DATES
1	February 4th through March 4th
2	March 5th through April 4th
3	April 5th through May 4th
4	May 5th through June 5th
5	June 6th through July 6th
6	July 7th through August 6th
7	August 7th through September 6th
8	September 7th through October 7th
9	October 8th through November 6th
10	November 7th through December 6th
11	December 7th through January 4th
12	January 5th through February 3rd

Use the following procedure to find your month star:

- Note your birth star on your Personal Data List.
- Note the Chinese month in which you were born.
- Find and note your month star using the appropriate table (one for men and one for women) as follows. You will find your birth star number at the left of the table and your Chinese month at the top. Your month star number is where the birth star row and the month star column intersect.

MONTH STARS FOR MEN

CHINESE MONTH	1	2	3	4	5	6	7	8	9	10	11	12
BIRTH STARS 1,4,7	8	7	6	5	4	3	2	1	9	8	7	6
3,6,9	5	4	3	2	1	9	8	7	6	5	4	3
2,5,8	2	1	9	8	7	6	5	4	3	2	1	9

For example, if you are a man born under 4 Wood Star during the second Chinese month, you have 7 Metal as your month star. If you are a man born under 3 Wood Star during the third Chinese month, your month star is 3 Wood Star.

MONTH STARS FOR WOMEN

CHINESE MONTH	1	2	3	4	5	6	7	8	9	10	11	12
BIRTH STARS 5,2,8	7	8	9	1	2	3	4	5	6	7	8	9
3,9,6	1	2	3	4	5	6	7	8	9	1	2	3
4,1,7	4	5	6	7	8	9	1	2	3	4	5	6

For example, if you are a woman born under 1 Water Star during the second Chinese month, your month star is 5 Earth Star. If you are a woman born under 9 Fire Star during the seventh Chinese month, your month star is 7 Metal Star.

FINDING YOUR TENDENCY STAR

Now that you have found your month star, use the following table to find your tendency star. Locate your birth star number at the top of the table and your month star number at the far left. Then locate your tendency star number in the body of the table where the birth star column and the month star row intersect.

TENDENCY STARS

BIRTH STARS	1	2	3	4	5	6	7	8	9
MONTH STARS 1	5	6	7	8	9	1	2	3	4
2	4	5	6	7	8	9	1	2	3
3	3	4	5	6	7	8	9	1	2
4	2	3	4	5	6	7	8	9	1
5	1	2	3	4	5	6	7	8	9
6	9	1	2	3	4	5	6	7	8
7	8	9	1	2	3	4	5	6	7
8	7	8	9	1	2	3	4	5	6
9	6	7	8	9	1	2	3	4	5

For example, if your birth star is 4 Wood Star and your month star is 7 Metal Star, your tendency star is 2 Earth Star. If your birth star is 1 Water Star and your month star is 5 Earth Star, your tendency star is 1 Water Star. If your birth star is 7 Metal Star and your month star is 4 Wood Star, your tendency star is 8 Earth Star.

THE EIGHTY-ONE PERSONALITY TYPES

There are eighty-one combinations of the birth, month, and tendency stars. These combinations constitute eighty-one personality types. This section will describe each personality type. One of them is yours. Each is labeled by a number combination, such as 1-1-5, 1-2-4, 1-3-3, and so on. These combinations are arranged birth star first, month star second, and tendency star third. For example, if your birth star is 1 Water Star, your month star is 1 Water Star, and your tendency star is 5 Earth Star, read the description for the number combination 1-1-5. If your birth star is 1 Water Star, your month star is 2 Earth Star, and your tendency star is 4 Wood Star, read the description for the number combination 1-2-4, and so forth.

Please note: If you have 5 Earth Star as your tendency star, you have an additional tendency star, which is indicated in your number combination description.

1 - 1 - 5   Your success depends on being resolute. You are a perfectionist and are
ambitious. When in a position of power you can become something of a task-
master, caring little for the ideas and feelings of those under you. Although
you are generally lucky, you need to cultivate tact. You are restless by nature.
You can be a good teacher and have artistic abilities. True success may come
relatively late in life; you are prone to changing your job and address frequently in earlier years. Your personality, being complex, has the tendencies
of both 5 Earth Star and 9 Fire Star. Read the descriptions of these stars on
pages 33 and 31.

1 - 2 - 4   Your success depends on perseverance. You are hardworking and detail
oriented. Naturally optimistic about the future, you dedicate much time and
energy to creating secure conditions for yourself and your loved ones. You are
a good organizer and are true to your ideals, even though your emotional vulnerability can plague you with doubts. You may be slow about making up
your mind, but once you do you will not change it easily. Although you are
sociable, you tend to be somewhat reserved, preferring to keep at a safe dis-
tance from all but those with whom you are closely involved. Even though
you have a talent for diplomacy, you need to cultivate the ability to understand the ideas and opinions of others. If you don't, you will be placing
unnecessary obstacles in your way. Your personality has the tendencies of 4
Wood Star. Read the description of this star on page 30.

1 - 3 - 3   Your success depends on being true to your ideals. Although you are normally a calm and sensitive person, you are capable of expressing yourself in a
surprisingly aggressive manner that not only offends others but leaves you
open to having your own feelings hurt. Once your feelings are hurt, you can
break off relations. This does not bode well for success in the business world.
You need to be aware of your shortcomings and to learn to cultivate patience
and adaptability. You have strong likes and dislikes and tend to throw yourself
wholeheartedly into what you do, striving almost obsessively to reach your
goal. You have the ability to motivate and inspire people, and you are gen-
uinely concerned about the well-being of others. Because you are honest,

high-spirited, enterprising, and inventive, you are generally fortunate in life. Your personality has the tendencies of 3 Wood Star. Read the description of this star on page 29.

1 - 4 - 2   Your success depends on not forcing your way against untoward conditions and opposition. Cultivate self-restraint and patience. You tend to be self-involved and opinionated, and have high expectations of other people. You have to clearly state your needs to others; if you don't people will misunderstand you. Concentrate on cultivating communication skills. You are hardworking and independent by nature and desire to be a leader. Notwithstanding, you are really at your best working under someone else. You are dependable, although somewhat indecisive, and would do well to find a job or position that you can hold for a long time. Your personality has the tendencies of 2 Earth Star. Read the description of this star on page 33.

1 - 5 - 1   Your success depends on perseverance and patience. Exercise careful restraint, and avoid gossip and useless arguing. Let your enemies defeat themselves. Do not allow your tendency to worry to get the best of you. You are serious-minded and self-protective but tend to doubt yourself. You thrive where others support you. You are sociable and creative, and work well as a member of a group. Your ambition and ability to work hard will bring you financial success. You can use your natural social skills to advantage in the area of sales. Because 1 Water Star is your tendency star as well as your birth star, your personality is most typical of 1 Water Star.

1 - 6 - 9   Your success depends on hard work. You are a natural leader. You tend to be independent and proud, and have great powers of concentration. You are slow to make decisions, weighing all sides carefully and keeping your own counsel. When you do make up your mind, you act in a straightforward and forceful manner, which can confuse and offend other people because you care to neither explain your motives nor compromise. You can be demanding, impatient, and hard to please. Although you are generally lucky, your pride stands in the way of your becoming a diplomat, and your independence may

cause you to change jobs frequently. Your personality has the tendencies of 9 Fire Star. Read the description of this star on page 31.

1-7-8   Your success depends on your ability to discriminate between what is true and what is false, and to make effective decisions. Reflect carefully to avoid going after empty illusions. You may tend to change jobs again and again until you find the one that best suits you. You need to be surrounded by intelligent, productive, and supportive co-workers, for even though you are hardworking, self-motivated, and assertive, your sensitivity causes you to doubt yourself too much. There may be extreme ups and downs on your career path. Your personality has the tendencies of 8 Earth Star. Read the description of this star on page 34.

1-8-7   Your success depends on securely establishing yourself. You have fine social and communication skills, which you can use to your benefit in any situation. You are generally optimistic and resourceful, and can take advantage of the friendliness you inspire in others to further a good cause. Although hardworking and a shrewd financial planner, you have a great capacity for enjoyment and will spend your money freely. You tend to be fickle and may find it difficult to make decisions and to keep your word. You are a skillful politician and diplomat. You may have several hobbies. Your personality has the tendencies of 7 Metal Star. Read the description of this star on page 36.

1-9-6   Your success depends on how well you know yourself. The cause of all your difficulties lies entirely in yourself. You are often motivated by your moods, which, if you are unaware of them, can bring you into open conflict with others. Be careful to avoid making enemies unnecessarily. You are stubborn, independent, and creative, and you desire power. You may have a taste for gambling. Your personality has the tendencies of 6 Metal Star. Read the description of this star on page 36.

2-1-6   Your success depends on cultivating sagacity. Guard against deception. Be careful not to place your trust in others too readily. Although you have considerable pride, you are dependent by nature and need to feel safe and secure in a partnership. If your partners are untrustworthy, you will meet with misfortune. You tend to be self-sacrificing. You may also tend to have narrow views or to view the world through rose-colored glasses, which makes it rather difficult for you to see things as they really are. Your personality has the tendencies of 6 Metal Star. Read the description of this star on page 36.

2 - 2 - 5   Your success comes as the result of slow accumulation. Follow the examples of the most successful people in your field. You are extremely cautious and conservative, and tend to be stubborn. There are two opposite tendencies in your character: the desire to lead and the need to follow. You can rise to a high position in your career, but if your need to be in control gets the best of you, you will suffer serious setbacks along the way. Because you are faithful by nature, you are destined either to follow someone else or to devote yourself to a great cause. You need the support of others to become successful. In your early years your conflicting desires may cause you to change address and job frequently. As a result, true success will come relatively late in your career. Your personality, being complex, has the tendencies of both 5 Earth Star and 6 Metal Star. Read the descriptions of these stars on pages 33 and 36.

2 - 3 - 4   Your success depends on being at the leading edge of your field. You are perceptive and astute, and have a natural talent for strategy, which you can use to its fullest advantage in helping others attain their objectives. You are capable of taking on great responsibilities and of rising to a high position in government or business. The broader your outlook, the greater your success. You have excellent chances of building up your fortunes as long as you favor your conservative side and control your extravagant impulses. You are generally trustworthy. Your personality has the tendencies of 4 Wood Star. Read the description of this star on page 30.

2 - 4 - 3   Your success depends on being at the leading edge of your field. Although you are impulsive and energetic and appear independent, you cannot go too far on your own without needing help. You may find it difficult to

44

complete what you begin if you don't have the encouragement and support of others. But you can be a valuable asset, especially where you use your natural intuitive abilities. Your hunches are often right. You are honest, enthusiastic, and inventive, and are generally fortunate. Your personality has the tendencies of 3 Wood Star. Read the description of this star on page 29.

2 - 5 - 2 Your success comes as the result of gradual development. Follow the examples of the most successful people in your field. You are conservative and detail oriented, and have the ability to serve. You are hardworking and can devote full attention to your goal, which you will reach most easily if you show humility. You are at your best where you can feel safe and secure. You are naturally compliant and kindhearted, and need to be in a position that you can keep for a long time. Because 2 Earth Star is your tendency star as well as your birth star, your personality is most typical of 2 Earth Star. Read the description of this star on page 33.

2 - 6 - 1 Your success depends on creative thinking. You are highly sensitive and tend to be indecisive and dependent on others even though you desire authority. If you develop your powers of discrimination and attract people who are trustworthy and helpful to you, you will rise to a high position. You are acquisitive and detail oriented, and need to be where you can work under the same boss, or with the same partner, for a long time. Your personality has the tendencies of 1 Water Star. Read the description of this star on page 27.

2 - 7 - 9 Your success depends on maintaining a good reputation. Cultivate courage and leadership skills. If you attain a high position and are careless, you will attract the resentment of others. You are a good idea person and problem solver, and have excellent organizational abilities, preferring others to do the work. You can be very effective behind the scenes as an adviser to someone in a more powerful position. You tend to be restless and independent, and may change jobs many times or have more than one career. You are a creative thinker and a gifted teacher. Your personality has the tendencies of 9 Fire Star. Read the description of this star on page 31.

45

2 - 8 - 8 Cooperation is necessary for your success. You are ambitious and determined, and will rise to a position of great influence with the cooperation of your superiors. However, it is not always easy for you to be cooperative. You can behave reactively. Although you normally appear calm, you can become rudely aggressive, alienating others with your explosive temper. You have something of a dual personality. Your contradictory impulses, coupled with your skepticism, can cause you to change your mind unexpectedly, make serious errors of judgment, and lose your opportunities. Your career could be marked by extreme ups and downs. Try to cultivate steadiness and patience. Your personality has the tendencies of 8 Earth Star. Read the description of this star on page 34.

2 - 9 - 7 Your success depends on how alert to opportunity you are. You are a creative, intellectual, and social type, and can be an effective speaker. You have the ability to understand and relate to all sorts of people. You are a natural diplomat and can easily attract people into your life who will gladly help you attain success. Although you tend to be somewhat moody, you are generally easygoing and pleasure loving. You are generally open-minded and a good judge of character, and you can set high standards, which others gladly follow. Your personality has the tendencies of 7 Metal Star. Read the description of this star on page 36.

3 - 1 - 7 Your success depends on your ability to back off. Be cautious. Let go of weak people and follow the strong. You are a natural diplomat and an effective speaker. Your outlook is generally optimistic, and when you know what you want you will work hard to attain it. But if you become discontented you easily abandon what you are doing. You thrive in partnership. You are generally fortunate and easygoing, and love to be entertained. Your personality has the tendencies of 7 Metal Star. Read the description of this star on page 36.

3 - 2 - 6 Your success depends on perseverance, especially in hard times. You are a talented planner, organizer, and leader, and are capable of taking on responsibilities and rising to a high position, from which you can be of help to others.

You are very positive about your decisions and prefer to act independently. Partnerships are difficult for you because you tend to be impatient and stubborn. Your personality has the tendencies of 6 Metal Star. Read the description of this star on page 36.

3-3-5   Your success depends on being resourceful. Avoid overburdening yourself; too many pressures only hinder you. Your life, especially in your early years, is fraught with changes. You could change your residence and job frequently, and may even change your career. For this reason true success will come relatively late in life. You are adaptable and inventive, and have a natural aptitude for strategic planning. You also have the strange luck of gaining through seemingly unfortunate circumstances. Try to control your tendencies to be impulsive and restless because they can undermine you. If you cultivate courage and flexibility, you will gain the respect of others and will ultimately attain a high position both professionally and financially. You are generally sincere and trustworthy. Your personality, being complex, has the tendencies of both 5 Earth Star and 4 Wood Star. Read the descriptions of these stars on pages 33 and 30.

3-4-4   Your success depends on focusing. You are optimistic, intelligent, and inventive, and while you have a natural talent for planning, you may lack the perseverance to see your plans through. Your mind abounds with seemingly contradictory ideas that may give others the impression you are unreliable. However, you can always be trusted to act on your word once you have made up your mind. You need to cultivate steadiness. Your personality has the tendencies of 4 Wood Star. Read the description of this star on page 30.

3-5-3   Your success depends on turning adverse circumstances into opportunities. Cultivate patience, perseverance, and humility. You are assertive, are a fast learner, and tend to be impulsive. Your impulsive tendencies can cause you a lot of unnecessary trouble. You may leave projects unfinished, rise meteorically only to burn out, or attempt to force your way against insurmountable odds only to run out of luck. Nonetheless, if you control your impulses and take advantage of your natural ability to create long-range plans, you will become completely successful. You can be a persuasive talker and are honest and straightforward in manner. Avoid anger. Because 3 Wood Star is your tendency star as well as your birth star, your personality is most typical of 3 Wood Star. Read the description of this star on page 29.

3 - 6 - 2 Your success depends on how well you know yourself. Develop your inner resources and exercise self-discipline. Independent, strong willed, and courageous, you need to express yourself creatively. You have great talent to plan and organize and enjoy working hard to accomplish your aims. Although you tend to be inflexible, impatient, and proud, you are kind-hearted, intuitive, and interested in the welfare of others. You are happiest in an interesting job that you can keep for a long time. Your personality has the tendencies of 2 Earth Star. Read the description of this star on page 33.

3 - 7 - 1 Your success depends on diligence. You will benefit by planning ahead and waiting for the right conditions before you take action. You may receive little help or encouragement in the early years of your career, but your situation eventually turns around, enabling you to rise to a fortunate position. Avoid impatience. You are sensitive and may be put off and discouraged by the negative remarks of others. Always keep in mind that perseverance wins out. Your personality has the tendencies of 1 Water Star. Read the description of this star on page 27.

3 - 8 - 9 Your success depends on being realistic. Be certain about what you want to accomplish and what it requires of you, and weigh that against your abilities and resources. Your lot may not always be an easy one. However, if you are prepared to tackle the challenges you undertake, you will be successful. You have the ability to turn adverse conditions to your advantage. You are ambitious and proud, and desire to lead. You are highly creative and are a good teacher. You may be prone to change jobs frequently because you have little patience. Your personality has the tendencies of 9 Fire Star. Read the description of this star on page 31.

3 - 9 - 8 Your success depends on cultivating high aspirations. Consider how your work may benefit the world. The more broad-minded you become, the better your chances of success. You are capable of great vision and humanitarian works. Conversely, the more self-seeking you become, the more you will experience difficulties. If you give free rein to your moods, your life and career will be subject to extreme ups and downs. Your personality has the tendencies of 8 Earth Star. Read the description of this star on page 34.

4 - 1 - 8 Your success depends on avoiding rash decisions and on knowing when not to act. Criticizing the errors of others too hastily is a mistake. Being right is not enough for you. You find it difficult to compromise. You tend to be stubborn and inflexible, and can be quite intolerant of other people's errors. You can act rashly and can step on others' toes without considering the consequences. Something of a reformer, you will attract both powerful friends and powerful enemies. Your career is subject to extreme ups and downs. Your personality has the tendencies of 8 Earth Star. Read the description of this star on page 34.

4 - 2 - 7 Your success depends on overcoming your ambivalence and taking decisive action. Cultivate your talents, and let your inspiration guide you. You are both softhearted and shrewd. Depending on how you balance these qualities, either your career path will be frustrated or you will attain a high position. If you combine your sensitivity with your shrewdness, you will become an expert diplomat with great predictive abilities. You are a persuasive talker and love entertainment. Your finances generally improve as you grow older. Your personality has the tendencies of 7 Metal Star. Read the description of this star on page 36.

4 - 3 - 6 Your success depends on unwavering perseverance. Like an expert navigator, always be willing to check and correct your course. Your feelings often lead you to have biased judgment. Avoid reckless attempts to succeed. If you take on more than you can handle, or find your way into a position that demands more skill or knowledge than you can muster, you will run into seri-

ous difficulties. You tend to be proud and stubborn on the one hand and tenderhearted on the other. You have natural leadership abilities and can work effectively in a corporate environment. Your personality has the tendencies of 6 Metal Star. Read the description of this star on page 36.

4 - 4 - 5 Your success depends on overcoming your tendency to vacillate. Because of your impatience, your life and career may be full of changes, especially in your early years. For this reason true success for you does not come until relatively late in life. Be careful that your need to be admired does not open you to deception. Others can and will mislead you. Your personality, being complex, has the tendencies of both 5 Earth Star and 3 Wood Star. Read the descriptions of these stars on pages 33 and 29.

4 - 5 - 4 Your success depends on turning adversity to opportunity. This does not mean trying to force your way against insurmountable odds, however, unless you are out for trouble! You tend to be willful, determined, and impulsive on the one hand and changeable and indecisive on the other. In your indecision you can resort to ferreting out secret motives and questioning everything until you lose your ability to decide. You need to cultivate farsightedness. You are generally trustworthy and like the company of others. You are also diplomatic and enjoy traveling. Because 4 Wood Star is your tendency star as well as your birth star, your personality is most typical of 4 Wood Star. Read the description of this star on page 30.

4 - 6 - 3 Your success depends on the ability to be resolute, patient, and consistent. Vacillating leads to failure. You tend to be strongly influenced by your emotions. Either you will work with great enthusiasm or you will totally lose interest in what you are doing, depending on how you feel about the people with whom you are working. Because you tend to be somewhat naive, you are open to suggestion and can be misled. It is sometimes difficult for you to see things objectively. You are quick to anger when you feel let down. You are generally honest. Your personality has the tendencies of 3 Wood Star. Read the description of this star on page 29.

4-7-2 Your success depends on how well you know yourself. Develop your inner resources. Your sincerity and good faith invariably attract good fortune. You are generally kindhearted, yielding, and considerate, and because of your sensitivity are vulnerable to criticism and misunderstanding. You tend to be extremely meticulous in your work and have the ability to lead others by example. It is best for you to find a line of work or position that you can keep for a long time. Your personality has the tendencies of 2 Earth Star. Read the description of this star on page 33.

4-8-1 Your success depends on creating secure conditions for others as well as for yourself. Cultivate a humanitarian view that is grounded in positive faith. The more you work for the universal good, the more you will prosper. You are hardworking and outspoken, and have the ability to influence others. If you neglect your inner work and relate to others out of insecurity and fear, your career will suffer, because you will become manipulative, self-centered, unable to make clear decisions, and resentful of the need to compromise. Your personality has the tendencies of 1 Water Star. Read the description of this star on page 27.

4-9-9 Your success depends on farsighted planning and the ability to take advantage of your opportunities. Cultivate positive faith and decisiveness. You have strong creative abilities and powers of expression, which you can use easily to influence others. You love to attract attention. If others fail to admire your mental brilliance and style, however, you can become quite upset. You tend to be volatile and proud, and find it difficult to behave diplomatically. Nonetheless, your farsightedness and creative imagination make you a good educator and artist. Your independence and changeability may cause you to switch jobs relatively frequently. Your personality has the tendencies of 9 Fire Star. Read the description of this star on page 31.

5-1-9 Your success depends on the cultivation of patience. Trying to make progress too quickly will lead to reversals. Avoid pettiness. If you attain a high position and behave in a careless, arrogant, or narrow-minded way, you will attract envy and draw misfortune on yourself. It is difficult for you to accept the views of others when they differ from your own. You do not care to compromise and will try to bend others to your will whenever possible. Your pride makes it difficult for you to behave diplomatically. However, your intelligence and creativity can make you a good teacher and artist. You have the ability to speak persuasively. Your independence may cause you to change jobs relatively frequently. Your personality has the tendencies of 9 Fire Star. Read the description of this star on page 31.

5 - 2 - 8   Your success depends on the cultivation of calmness. Always think before you act. Seek cooperation with others. You have great determination and will succeed in your career against all odds. You have a strong sense of honor and want to be appreciated. When other people think well of you you flourish, but you can become quite distressed when they ignore you or think ill of you. You need to be in control. For this reason your career may be subject to extreme ups and downs. Your personality has the tendencies of 8 Earth Star. Read the description of this star on page 34.

5 - 3 - 7   Your success depends on forward movement. Let go of the past! Cultivate definite goals, and strive for independence. Although you are strong willed and self-possessed, you tend to base your decisions on your feelings and allow yourself to be influenced by others, especially those who are close to you. For this reason you can easily lose sight of your goals. It is best for you to follow your spiritual impulses and do what you are inspired to do rather than what you think you ought to do. If you are completely dedicated to what you're doing, no one's opinion will deflect you. Your personality has the tendencies of 7 Metal Star. Read the description of this star on page 36.

5 - 4 - 6   Your success depends on forward movement. Don't look back! Develop leadership skills. Learn to cooperate with those above as well as below you, even when it seems difficult to adapt to conditions not to your liking. Consider that flexibility may be necessary at times if you are to attain the degree of leadership to which you aspire. You are proud and stubborn. Your

personality has the tendencies of 6 Metal Star. Read the description of this star on page 36.

5-5-5 Your success depends on being centered in yourself and attaining a key position in your professional circle. You need to be in perfect control of yourself and to create and maintain definite boundaries in order to be effective. You are entirely self-motivated and profoundly dedicated to your goals, which are often humanitarian. You are able to counsel others and take on great responsibilities. You can have a pivotal influence on the lives and careers of others. Because 5 Earth Star is your tendency star as well as your birth star and month star, your personality is most typical of 5 Earth Star. Read the description of this star on page 33.

5-6-4 Your success depends on knowing that good and bad luck are but two sides of a coin. Never lose faith. Keep an open mind. Although you are willful and determined, you can be discouraged and tempted to abandon your goals under adverse conditions. You need to cultivate enough flexibility to tide you over the difficult periods caused by circumstances beyond your control. You can be objective and are generally trustworthy. Your personality has the tendencies of 4 Wood Star. Read the description of this star on page 30.

5-7-3 Your success depends on knowing that good and bad luck give rise to each other. Be cautious. Pressing your luck invites misfortune. You tend to be intolerant of constraints and want to have your way no matter what the cost. Try to control your tendency to be impatient, which can cause you to abandon one project after another. You are straightforward, enthusiastic, and inventive. Your personality has the tendencies of 3 Wood Star. Read the description of this star on page 29.

5-8-2 Your success depends on cultivating receptivity. Do not attempt to lead when you should follow. Because of your need to be in control, you may appear stronger than you really are. You would do well, instead of trying to take the lead, to consider playing a supportive role. You are most secure when working for someone you admire. You are hardworking and diligent, and take pride in what you accomplish. Your personality has the tendencies of 2 Earth Star. Read the description of this star on page 33.

5 - 9 - 1 Your success depends on gratitude. Do not try to use force against obstacles. Your restlessness and discontentment may cause you to struggle through life. Driven by a desire for fame and fortune, you could attach yourself to one person after another, hoping that they might open doors and make connections for you. You must cultivate self-reliance and avoid trying to control other people through their feelings. You are lively and sociable, and are a persuasive talker. Your personality has the tendencies of 1 Water Star. Read the description of this star on page 27.

6 - 1 - 1 Your success depends on peaceful cooperation. Although your disposition is usually calm, you are emotionally vulnerable and can react violently when others express opinions at variance with your own. It is better for you to retreat when confronted with opposition and let matters take their course. You need the support of other people to realize your goals. Fighting only hinders you. You are a perfectionist by nature and are apt to reorganize your plans and projects again and again. Your personality has the tendencies of 1 Water Star. Read the description of this star on page 27.

6 - 2 - 9 Your success depends on contentment. Acting out of purely self-centered motives and boasting about your abilities and accomplishments will attract the ill will of others. Although you have the ability to lead, and the intelligence and creative talent to organize large projects, trying to force your way to the top could spell your downfall. Your pride makes it difficult for you to act with diplomacy. Your independence could bring you to change jobs relatively frequently. Your personality has the tendencies of 9 Fire Star. Read the description of this star on page 31.

6 - 3 - 8 Your success depends on circumspection. Always practice self-restraint. You are at your best working behind the scenes, masterminding large-scale

projects for others to execute. From time to time you may find yourself in a position of leadership, but because your life and career tend to run into surprising ups and downs, you should be willing to step down when necessary and adapt to new conditions. Your personality has the tendencies of 8 Earth Star. Read the description of this star on page 34.

6 - 4 - 7 Your success depends on developing your intuition. Expect the unexpected. Because you have an indomitable will and sense of true purpose, you can be a great leader in times of danger. You are a persuasive talker and natural diplomat, and can motivate and encourage others to take positive action by appealing to their emotions. You are highly sociable and need to be appreciated for your intelligence and quick wit. You have a strong sense of justice and are inclined to defend the underdog. Your personality has the tendencies of 7 Metal Star. Read the description of this star on page 36.

6 - 5 - 6 Your success depends on the gradual cultivation of your inner resources. If you climb too far too fast, you will become isolated and undone. You are creative and ambitious, and aim to be a leader. You generally hate to listen to advice or to make compromises and will not consider the needs of others unless they are instrumental to your aims. Being something of a gambler you are capable of taking great risks in your life and career. Because 6 Metal Star is your tendency star as well as your birth star, your personality is most typical of 6 Metal Star.

6 - 6 - 5 Your success depends on timely action. Be steady in your aim and flexible in your attitudes as you meet the difficult challenges of your career. Your life, especially in your early years, may be full of changes. You may change your address and job many times, and may even change your career. For this reason true success comes relatively late. Although it is difficult for you to accept the ideas and advice of others, you have talent as an arbitrator and peacemaker. Although you have pride, you tend to be kindhearted. You enjoy working with others. Your personality, being complex, has the tendencies of both 5 Earth Star and 2 Earth Star. Read the descriptions of these stars on page 33.

6 - 7 - 4 Your success depends on being mindful of boundaries. Don't bite off more than you can chew. Do not overstep your limits and attempt to do what is beyond your ability; to do so will only lead to misfortune. Rely on common sense. Know when to stop and when to correct your course. You are hardworking and detail oriented, and have the natural ability to lead others. Your personality has the tendencies of 4 Wood Star. Read the description of this star on page 30.

6 - 8 - 3 Your success depends on self-reliance. Be cautious in your pursuit and use of power. You are a natural leader. If you proceed step by step, paying attention to details while cultivating an open mind, you will see all obstacles fall away in time. Try to control the impulsive and impatient side of your personality. You can be enthusiastic and outspoken, and your mind can overflow with interesting ideas. Your personality has the tendencies of 3 Wood Star. Read the description of this star on page 29.

6 - 9 - 2 Your success depends on keeping your aim steady while adapting to changing conditions. You have talent as an arbitrator and peacemaker, and enjoy working for others who are in a position of authority. You will do your best in a position that you can hold for a long time. Although you are strong willed, you are kindhearted. You are hardworking, diligent, and detail oriented. Your personality has the tendencies of 2 Earth Star. Read the description of this star on page 33.

7 - 1 - 2 Your success depends on cultivating humane conduct. Follow the golden rule. You are a natural peacemaker and organizer. You are kindhearted and sociable, and have strong intuitive abilities. You also have the knack of attracting people who bring you luck. Even though you are an independent thinker, you are at your best where you can work under someone you respect and admire. You prefer to have a job that you can keep for a long time. Your personality has the tendencies of 2 Earth Star. Read the description of this star on page 33.

7-2-1 Your success depends on viewing the negative behavior of others with equanimity. You are highly sensitive, questioning, and resourceful. An astute conversationalist and listener, you weigh different sides of an issue carefully and take a long time to make up your mind; you do not trust easily. Your decisions and insights can surprise others. You love to be entertained and thrive where you work among supportive and enthusiastic people. But where others are unsupportive and out of harmony with you, you tend to lose interest in the projects at hand. Be that as it may, you always succeed by shrewd planning and perseverance. You have excellent social skills and artistic taste. Your personality has the tendencies of 1 Water Star. Read the description of this star on page 27.

7-3-9 Your success depends on an optimistic outlook. Seek out cooperative and trustworthy partners. Although you may face difficult conditions early in your career, your efforts will be crowned with success later. Although you can leave one job after another out of frustration, you have the ability to hold on through challenging conditions. You need to work where you can exercise your creative intelligence in a free and positive way in order to feel happy. You are a persuasive talker, are highly sociable, and have the ability to attract powerful allies when in need of help. Your personality has the tendencies of 9 Fire Star. Read the description of this star on page 31.

7-4-8 Your success depends on cultivating balance and harmony. If you learn to modify your tendencies to be opinionated and unyielding, you could benefit greatly by going into business with a partner. You may experience extreme ups and downs in your life and career because of your hypersensitivity. Don't cut off your nose to spite your face! Your personality has the tendencies of 8 Earth Star. Read the description of this star on page 34.

7-5-7 Your success depends on knowing what you want and going for it. You have the ability to pursue an independent career. Being a persuasive talker and talented diplomat, you can bring the right people together with little trouble whenever you need to. It is easy for you to lead others when you are clear about your goals. You are a hard worker and are generally thorough. Because 7 Metal Star is your tendency star as well as your birth star, your personality is most typical of 7 Metal Star. Read the description of this star on page 36.

7 - 6 - 6 Your success depends on quiet persistence. Be resolute, not relentless. Although you are capable of showing great dignity and self-confidence, you can shock others by blowing up when you feel offended by imagined slights. You are idealistic and tend to judge others by high standards. If you go through life unaware of yourself, you will only undermine your progress. Notwithstanding, you have the natural ability to lead. Your personality has the tendencies of 6 Metal Star. Read the description of this star on page 36.

7 - 7 - 5 Your success depends on seizing your opportunities. You have talents for directing and arbitrating. You are a peacemaker and have the ability to attract helpful partners whenever you need them. You are capable of organizing large-scale projects in great detail and of working hard to see them through. Notwithstanding, your vulnerability to criticism, especially in early years, can cause extreme ups and downs in your life and career. For this reason true success comes relatively late in life. Your personality, being complex, has the tendencies of both 5 Earth Star and 8 Earth Star. Read the descriptions of these stars on pages 33 and 34.

7 - 8 - 4 Your success depends on perseverance. You are a gifted peacemaker and have excellent social skills. You are flexible, trustworthy, and considerate, and are capable of taking on great responsibilities. A natural diplomat, you are a most persuasive talker who can inspire enthusiasm in others. Your personality has the tendencies of 4 Wood Star. Read the description of this star on page 30.

7 - 9 - 3 Your success depends on waiting for good opportunities to appear. Never resort to inappropriate measures or to acting out of impatience or shortsightedness. If you do you will run into trouble. Your need for attention allows others to take advantage of you. You are susceptible to flattery. Try to form a

partnership with someone who can understand and tolerate the duality of your nature. You are positively outgoing on the one hand and vulnerable, especially to criticism, on the other. You are generally straightforward and enthusiastic but can be quick to anger. Your personality has the tendencies of 3 Wood Star. Read the description of this star on page 29.

8 - 1 - 3   Your success depends on self-confidence. You tend to be impatient and always want to be on the go. This, of course, can bring much turmoil and frustration into your life and career. But because you are determined to have your way, you will attain your goals in the long run. Experience is your best teacher. You are generally honest and straightforward but need to control your tendency to be impatient and irritable. Your personality has the tendencies of 3 Wood Star. Read the description of this star on page 29.

8 - 2 - 2   Your success depends on the accumulation of merit. Cultivate humility and modesty in all your dealings. Although you have the ability to lead, it is best for you to work under someone you can trust. It is also best for you to work for the universal good, because you have the natural ability to benefit others through service. Although your disposition is generally mild, you can blow up quite suddenly under pressure. You need to consider the effect that might have on others. Your personality has the tendencies of 2 Earth Star. Read the description of this star on page 33.

8 - 3 - 1   Your success depends on not underestimating yourself. Your winning qualities are ambition and patience. Whatever you truly desire you will ultimately attain. You love to be continuously active and are happiest where you can work at a job that has a variety of activities. You are capable of developing a business that starts out small and becomes very large. You have a natural talent for sales. Your personality has the tendencies of 1 Water Star. Read the description of this star on page 27.

8 - 4 - 9   Your success depends on making wise choices. Keep your long-range goals clearly in mind, and avoid wasting time on trivial matters. Because you

tend to be restless, changeability characterizes your life. You can easily change your plans, your job, and your address. How you understand and make changes is of critical importance to your progress. If you are not clear about your goals and precipitate changes for the wrong reasons, you will lose ground. However, if you subordinate your tendency to change to your long-range goal, you will attain what you want. You have the ability to be a leader. Your personality has the tendencies of 9 Fire Star. Read the description of this star on page 31.

8 - 5 - 8   Your success depends on following the examples of great figures from the past. Pay attention to your inner development. If you attain inner peace, regardless of your material circumstances you will meet with good fortune. You need to work at balancing your energies, because you have strongly opposing tendencies, which can bring you to experience many extreme ups and downs in your life and career. Be careful not to scatter your attention and energies by pursuing several divergent goals at the same time. You dislike having to remain in the same place doing the same thing for long. You would do well as a freelancer. Because 8 Earth Star is your tendency star as well as your birth star, your personality is most typical of 8 Earth Star. Read the description of this star on page 34.

8 - 6 - 7   Your success depends on pursuing your goals with enthusiasm. Strive to be flexible in your thinking. If you become too rigid and opinionated, you will have cause for regret. You can be strong willed and imperious on the one hand and easygoing on the other. You are a persuasive talker and have a talent for diplomacy. You are generally hardworking and can make decisions at lightning speed because you are highly intuitive. Your personality has the tendencies of 7 Metal Star. Read the description of this star on page 36.

8 - 7 - 6   Your success depends on following the golden rule. Contemplate the meanings of cooperation. You have the ability to lead others. You are a good organizer and are detail oriented but tend to become inflexible, demanding, and judgmental. Although you may appear easygoing, you are strong willed

and stubborn, and will not change your mind once you have come to a deci-sion. Your personality has the tendencies of 6 Metal Star. Read the descrip-tion of this star on page 36.

8 - 8 - 5 Your success depends on keeping a clear and steady course. Strive to become independent. You are ambitious and restless, and have an adventur-ous spirit, which brings many changes into your life. You may change resi-dence and jobs many times, especially in your early years, and may change your career several times. You can also overwork by taking on more than you can handle at once. For these reasons true success comes relatively late in your life. You are an effective speaker and have a talent for diplomacy. Your personality, being complex, has the tendencies of both 5 Earth Star and 7 Metal Star. Read the descriptions of these stars on pages 33 and 36.

8 - 9 - 4 Your success depends on taking control of your emotions. Learn from your mistakes, and cultivate positive faith in the face of difficulties. Because you tend to be emotionally changeable and strong willed, you can become reckless. If you don't want your life and career to fall into turmoil, become aware of yourself and learn to control your tendency to doubt. You often base your decisions on your feelings. On a positive note, you are happiest in a job that allows for change, variety, and travel. Your personality has the tendencies of 4 Wood Star. Read the description of this star on page 30.

9 - 1 - 4 Your success depends on diligence. Be cooperative and aware of the needs of others. The more you care for others and are of service, the happier and more prosperous you will be. You are zealous and far seeing, and have the ability to be a leader. However, you can go too far in your zeal and become so intolerant of the wishes of others that those you would lead will rebel against you. You need to control your impulsiveness and pride. Your personality has the tendencies of 4 Wood Star. Read the description of this star on page 30.

9 - 2 - 3 Your success depends on patience. You are straightforward, enthusiastic, and inventive, and have great expectations of life. You tend to pursue your

aims aggressively and impatiently, and can become manipulative and explosive in the face of obstacles. You need to control your irritability. You love to attract attention and need the support of others to make effective progress in your career. Your personality has the tendencies of 3 Wood Star. Read the description of this star on page 29.

9 - 3 - 2   Your success depends on calmly biding your time and seizing the right moment to take action. Be vigilant. Your ambition is strong; you need to control it, not let it control you. Think of your aspiration as a bow and arrow; if you are good at controlling the tension, you will always hit the mark. You can hold an administrative position in an area of public service or government. Your personality has the tendencies of 2 Earth Star. Read the description of this star on page 33.

9 - 4 - 1   Your success depends on knowing when to wait and when to retreat. Do not resort to inappropriate means or cunning to have your way. You tend to be restless and changeable, and are easily bored. You don't like waiting. Be practical. You will reach your goals more quickly if you take your time. You need to be appreciated for your abilities and talents. Cultivate your social and conversational skills. Your personality has the tendencies of 1 Water Star. Read the description of this star on page 27.

9 - 5 - 9   Your success depends on being clear minded and certain of what you want. You are creative and visionary, and have the ability to be a leader and reformer. Your ability to lead others may be difficult to realize, however, because you are volatile, quick to anger, and apt to change your mind without considering the feelings of others. Your need to be in control often prevents you from exercising tact. Try to cultivate patience. Your need for independence could lead you to change jobs relatively often. Because 9 Fire Star is your tendency star as well as your birth star, your personality is most characteristic of 9 Fire Star.

9-6-8 Your success depends on being consistent. You are generally self-motivated and ambitious, and have excellent powers of concentration. You need to be firmly in control of your situation and to rise swiftly to the leading position. If you meet with opposition, you will fight, even violently, to have your way. However, if circumstances beyond your control force you to slow down, your feelings may suddenly cause you to lose interest in what you are doing. For this reason you are likely to experience extreme ups and downs in your life and career. You need to be considerate of others. Your personality has the tendencies of 8 Earth Star. Read the description of this star on page 34.

9-7-7 Your success depends on enduring hardships. Know what you want and prepare for it. When the time is right, act and you will be successful. Although you have excellent organizational abilities and are generally easy-going, you can sabotage your plans by blowing up under pressure. You do not take stress well. On the other hand, you have an excellent talent for diplomacy and are a persuasive talker. You attract friends and allies easily. Your personality has the tendencies of 7 Metal Star. Read the description of this star on page 36.

9-8-6 Your success depends on taking one step at a time. Cultivate sincerity. If you try to make progress while secretly mistrusting others, you will only succeed in causing others to mistrust you. You are proud and stubborn, and can be ruthless in your quest for power. Be careful! On a positive note, you are a perfectionist and a leader with strong organizational abilities. Your personality has the tendencies of 6 Metal Star. Read the description of this star on page 36.

9-9-5 Your success depends on being resolute. In spite of the fact that you are far seeing, you lack sufficient patience to organize your affairs to your best advantage. Your restless nature can cause you to change jobs and addresses frequently, especially in your early years. You could also change careers several times. For these reasons true success comes relatively late in your life. You are an active and sociable type, and are prone to many changes of mood. Your personality, being complex, has the tendencies of both 5 Earth Star and 1 Water Star. Read the descriptions of these stars on pages 33 and 27.

EXERCISE

On your Personal Data List:

- Write down your month star and its element.
- Write down the yin or yang quality of your month star.
- Write down the month stars of your significant others.
- Write down your tendency star and its element.
- Write down the yin or yang quality of your tendency star.
- Write down the tendency stars of your significant others.

If you need help in remembering the elements and yin and yang qualities of the stars, refer to the table "The Nine Stars" on page 23.

- To determine your predominant element, look at the elements of your season of birth, your birth star, your month star, and your tendency star. Whichever occurs most often is the predominant element of your personality and will indicate something about your talents and a possible career direction. Once you have determined your predominant element, refer to the descriptions of businesses and aptitudes in Chapter 1. If your tally shows no predominant element—if, for example, you were born in the summer (the Fire season) of a 3 Wood Star year, in a month of 1 Water Star, and with 7 Metal Star as your tendency star—you have no predominant element. In this case simply give your tendency star the strongest emphasis. Write down your predominant element on your Personal Data List.
- To determine your predominant yin or yang quality, look at the yin or yang qualities of your season of birth, your birth star, your month star, and your

tendency star. Whichever occurs most often will reveal whether your personality is predominantly yin or yang, or a balance of the two. The yin personality is better suited to working quietly behind the scenes, while the yang personality is better suited to working more actively out in the world.

chapter 4

YOUR
LUCKY STARS

Now that you know your birth star, month star, and tendency star, let's look at your lucky stars. Your lucky stars, even more than your birth star, reveal the best directions in space to which you should align your furniture. Your lucky stars also reveal the lucky colors, shapes, and patterns you should use for decorating your office or workplace, creating your personal business logo, and designing signs. You can also wear your lucky colors.

Note on the following table that your lucky stars are derived from the combination of your birth star and your month star.

FINDING YOUR LUCKY STARS

Referring to your Personal Data List, note your birth star and month star. Then look through the table of lucky stars. Where you find your birth star and month star together, you will also find your lucky star, or stars. For example, if your birth star is 1 Water Star and your month star is 1 Water Star, your lucky stars are 3 Wood Star, 4 Wood Star, 6 Metal Star, and 7 Metal Star. If your birth star is 3 Wood Star and your month star is 9 Fire Star, your lucky star is 4 Wood Star.

Remember, the elements of the stars are 1 Water, 2 Earth, 3 Wood, 4 Wood, 5 Earth, 6 Metal, 7 Metal, 8 Earth, 9 Fire.

LUCKY STARS

Birth Star	Month Star	Lucky Stars
1	1	3, 4, 6, 7
1	2	6, 7
1	3	4
1	4	3
1	5	6, 7
1	6	7
1	7	6
1	8	6, 7
1	9	3, 4
2	1	6, 7
2	2	5, 6, 7, 8, 9
2	3	9
2	4	9
2	5	6, 7, 8
2	6	5, 7, 8
2	7	5, 6, 8
2	8	5, 6, 7, 9
2	9	5, 8
3	1	4
3	2	9
3	3	1, 4, 9
3	4	1, 9
3	5	9
3	6	1
3	7	1
3	8	9
3	9	4
4	1	3
4	2	9
4	3	1, 9
4	4	1, 3, 9
4	5	9

BIRTH STAR	MONTH STAR	LUCKY STARS
4	6	1
4	7	1
4	8	9
4	9	3
5	1	6, 7
5	2	6, 7, 8, 9
5	3	9
5	4	9
5	5	2, 6, 7, 8, 9
5	6	2, 7, 8
5	7	2, 6, 8
5	8	2, 6, 7
5	9	2, 8
6	1	7
6	2	5, 7, 8
6	3	1
6	4	1
6	5	2, 7, 8
6	6	1, 2, 5, 7, 8
6	7	1, 2, 5, 8
6	8	2, 5, 7
6	9	2, 5, 8
7	1	6
7	2	5, 6, 8
7	3	1
7	4	1
7	5	2, 6, 8
7	6	1, 2, 5, 8
7	7	1, 2, 5, 6, 8
7	8	2, 5, 6
7	9	2, 5, 8
8	1	6, 7
8	2	5, 6, 7, 9
8	3	9
8	4	9

Birth Star	Month Star	Lucky Stars
8	5	2, 6, 7, 9
8	6	2, 5, 7
8	7	2, 5, 6
8	8	2, 5, 6, 7, 9
8	9	2, 5
9	1	3, 4
9	2	5, 8
9	3	4
9	4	3
9	5	2, 8
9	6	2, 5, 8
9	7	2, 5, 8
9	8	2, 5
9	9	2, 3, 4, 5, 8

LUCKY STAR CORRESPONDENCES

Here is a special color scale for the lucky stars. It is more specific than the color ranges given in Chapter 1 for the five elements. You will find the lucky star color scale in the following table of lucky star correspondences. Note that corresponding directions in space, shapes, and patterns, as well as suggestive images are also included.

LUCKY STAR CORRESPONDENCES

Star	Direction in Space	Color	Shape	Pattern	Images
1 Water	North	White	Undulant, asymmetrical	Ripples Waves	Moon, reeds, clouds, lilies, goldfish
2 Earth	Southwest	Black	Square	Squares Cubes	Wheat, cattle

STAR	DIRECTION in SPACE	COLOR	SHAPE	PATTERN	IMAGES
3 Wood	East	Light green	Rectangle	Rectangles	Trees, bamboo, dragons, rising sun, an eagle, a peach
4 Wood	Southeast	Dark green	Rectangle	Rectangles	Trees, a snake, a crane, a cock, poppies
5 Earth	Southwest for men; northeast for women	Yellow	Square, cube	Squares, cruciform	A scale
6 Metal	Northwest	White	Round, oval	Circles, ovals	A tiger, a lion, horses, cars, airplanes, a castle, chrysanthemums
7 Metal	West	Red	Round, oval	Circles, ovals	Deer, sheep, a honeybee, a sunset, magnolias, gardenias
8 Earth	Northeast	White	Square	Squares, cubes	A dog, an ox, a castle, a gate, mountains
9 Fire	South	Purple	Triangle	Chevrons	Pheasants, peacocks, a phoenix, sun, lightning, arrows, maple trees, a heart

Here are a few examples to give you an idea of how you can use your lucky stars.

■ James, born on October 31st, 1963, has 1 Water Star for his birth star and 9 Fire Star for his month star. This gives him 3 Wood Star and 4 Wood Star for his lucky stars. With this information James finds that his office space allows him to position his desk so that he can sit with his back to the southeast, the direction of 4 Wood Star. He also decides to decorate his office in shades of green, because they correspond to both 3 Wood and 4 Wood Stars, and places a sculpture of a dragon, corresponding to 3 Wood Star, in the east corner of his office.

- Alice is beginning a new business. Born on June 1st, 1963, she has 5 Earth Star for her birth star and 1 Water Star for her month star. This gives her 6 Metal Star and 7 Metal Star for her lucky stars. With this information Alice decides to position her desk so that she can sit with her back to the northwest, the direction of 6 Metal Star, and decorates her office in whites with some touches of bright red, the colors of 6 Metal Star and 7 Metal Star, respectively. Alice also has a logo with a circular motif, corresponding to the element Metal, designed for her new business.

- Diana, born on January 19th, 1964, has 5 Earth Star for her birth star and 9 Fire Star for her month star. This gives her 2 Earth Star and 8 Earth Star for her lucky stars. With this information Diana decides to position her desk so that she can sit with her back to the southwest, the direction of 2 Earth Star. She decorates her office in white and black, the colors of 8 Earth Star, and 2 Earth Star, respectively. She hangs a picture of a sheaf of wheat, corresponding to 2 Earth Star, on the southwest wall of her office.

EXERCISE

On your Personal Data List:

- Write down your lucky star or stars.
- Write down the directions in space, colors, shapes, patterns, and images that correspond to your lucky star or stars.

Now that you have this information, resist the temptation to make decorating decisions. Wait until you have read and understood Part Two to make your final decisions about what colors you are going to use in your office or workplace and how you are going to position your desk and other furniture.

chapter 5

YOUR RELATIONSHIPS

There are nine basic personality types and eighty-one subtypes, as characterized by the nine birth stars and the eighty-one combinations of the birth stars, month stars, and tendency stars. Because each of the nine basic personality types is distinct from the others, each relates to the others in distinct ways. The harmony and discord of your relationships can be seen in the harmonious and discordant relations of your stars with the stars of others.

If you want to find out how you might relate to someone but don't know her or his exact date of birth, you will need at least the year of birth to determine basic personality type.

THE FOUR ASPECTS

There are four ways, or aspects, in which the stars relate to one another. Three of these aspects are harmonious, and one is discordant. They are as follows:

- Supportive (harmonious)
- Cooperative (harmonious)
- Attracting (harmonious)
- Conflicting (discordant)

Here are the aspects for each star:

STAR	ASPECTS
1 Water Star	Supported by 6 Metal Star and 7 Metal Star Supports 3 Wood Star and 4 Wood Star Cooperates with 1 Water Star Is attracted by 9 Fire Star Conflicts with 2 Earth Star, 5 Earth Star, and 8 Earth Star
2 Earth Star	Supported by 9 Fire Star Supports 6 Metal Star and 7 Metal Star Cooperates with 5 Earth Star Is attracted by 8 Earth Star Conflicts with 1 Water Star, 3 Wood Star, and 4 Wood Star
3 Wood Star	Supported by 1 Water Star Supports 9 Fire Star Cooperates with 4 Wood Star Is attracted by 7 Metal Star Conflicts with 6 Metal Star, 2 Earth Star, 5 Earth Star, and 8 Earth Star
4 Wood Star	Supported by 1 Water Star Supports 9 Fire Star Cooperates with 3 Wood Star Is attracted by 6 Metal Star Conflicts with 7 Metal Star, 2 Earth Star, 5 Earth Star, and 8 Earth Star
5 Earth Star	Supported by 9 Fire Star Supports 6 Metal Star and 7 Metal Star Cooperates with 2 Earth Star and 8 Earth Star Is attracted by 5 Earth Star Conflicts with 1 Water Star, 3 Wood Star, and 4 Wood Star

STAR	ASPECTS
6 Metal Star	Supported by 2 Earth Star, 5 Earth Star, and 8 Earth Star Supports 1 Water Star Cooperates with 7 Metal Star Is attracted by 4 Wood Star Conflicts with 3 Wood Star and 9 Fire Star
7 Metal Star	Supported by 2 Earth Star, 5 Earth Star, and 8 Earth Star Supports 1 Water Star Cooperates with 6 Metal Star Is attracted by 3 Wood Star Conflicts with 4 Wood Star and 9 Fire Star
8 Earth Star	Supported by 9 Fire Star Supports 6 Metal Star and 7 Metal Star Cooperates with 5 Earth Star Is attracted by 2 Earth Star Conflicts with 1 Water Star, 3 Wood Star, and 4 Wood Star
9 Fire Star	Supported by 3 Wood Star and 4 Wood Star Supports 2 Earth Star, 5 Earth Star, and 8 Earth Star Cooperates with 9 Fire Star Is attracted by 1 Water Star Conflicts with 6 Metal Star and 7 Metal Star

THE ASPECTS OF YOUR BIRTH STAR

Because your birth star represents your basic personality, the harmonious or discordant aspect it has with someone else's birth star reveals the fundamental energetic condition of your relationship. Someone whose birth star supports yours will give you support. Someone whose birth star is supported by yours will receive support from you. If your birth stars are in cooperation, you will give to each other and receive from each other most easily. If you are in a relationship with someone whose birth star is attracted by yours, you will seek to be in harmony. If you are in a relationship with someone whose birth star conflicts with yours, you will be challenged to learn from your differences, or go your separate ways. Notwithstanding, the success or failure of any relationship depends on how well both individuals understand themselves and each other. Even the most perfect astrological match can be ruined if you don't respect each other. As Shakespeare so aptly put it, "The fault, dear Brutus, is not in our stars, but in ourselves."

THE ASPECTS OF YOUR MONTH STAR

Your month star represents your mental disposition. The harmonious or discordant aspect it has with someone else's month star reveals how you communicate with each other. If you are in a relationship with someone whose month star supports your month star, you will receive ideas from him easily, as he is inclined to understand you. If you are in a relationship with someone whose month star is supported by yours, she will receive ideas from you easily as you are inclined to understand her. If you are in a relationship with someone whose month star is in cooperation with yours, you both will exchange ideas easily. If you are in a relationship with someone whose month star is attracted by yours, your communication will become most creative as you seek harmony together. If you are in a relationship with someone whose month star conflicts with yours, you both will entertain differences of opinion.

THE ASPECTS OF YOUR TENDENCY STAR

Your tendency star represents your attitude, or way of approaching the world. The harmonious or discordant aspect it has with someone else's tendency star reveals your outlooks. If you are in a relationship with someone whose tendency star supports yours, he will tend to support your views. If you are in a relationship with someone whose tendency star is supported by yours, you will tend to support her views. Someone whose tendency star is in cooperation with yours will tend to view life the same way you do. Someone whose tendency star is attracted by yours will seek a mutually agreeable relationship with you. If you are in a relationship with someone whose tendency star conflicts with yours, you will have trouble seeing eye to eye; you will agree to disagree.

The most harmonious of relationships, of course, is that in which the birth stars, month stars, and tendency stars of the two people are in harmony. Here are the stars for two people who have a most harmonious relationship:

	PERSON 1	PERSON 2
Birth star	3	4
Month star	3	7
Tendency star	5	2

In this relationship the birth stars are mutually cooperative, the month stars are mutually attractive, and the tendency stars are mutually cooperative. This shows that these two people energize each other, seeking to communicate creatively and harmoniously while sharing a common aim.

Here are the stars for two people in greatest conflict:

	PERSON 1	PERSON 2
Birth star	2	3
Month star	5	4
Tendency star	8	4

In this relationship the birth stars, month stars, and tendency stars are completely at variance. These two people have come together to learn from their differences.

REMEDIES FOR STARS IN CONFLICT

If you live, are in partnership, or share work space with someone whose birth star is in conflict with yours, you can put in the space you share or by your desk an object whose color corresponds to the element that mitigates the conflicting elements of your two stars. The following table shows all the problematic star combinations and their color remedies. Please note: When comparing your chart with someone else's, compare only birth star to birth star, month star to month star, and tendency star to tendency star.

PROBLEMATIC STAR COMBINATIONS AND MITIGATING COLORS

STAR OF PERSON 1	STAR OF PERSON 2	MITIGATING COLOR
1	2	White or silver
1	5	White or silver
1	8	White or silver
2	3	Red or purple
2	4	Red or purple
3	5	Red or purple
3	8	Red or purple
3	6	Black or navy
4	5	Red or purple
4	8	Red or purple
4	7	Black or navy
6	9	Yellow or orange
7	9	Yellow or orange

Jane, whose birth star is 3 Wood, and Robert, whose birth star is 5 Earth, share an office. They both find that they don't quite get along and that they tend to exhaust each other. Jane places a red vase in the office and keeps red and purple flowers in the vase. Robert finds this pleasing. The ice is broken, and soon after they begin to communicate more constructively.

THE FORTY-FIVE STAR RELATIONSHIP COMBINATIONS

1 WATER STAR WITH 1 WATER STAR

Because 1 Water Star cooperates with 1 Water Star, it is easy for you to relate to each other. However, since both of you are changeable and moody, you can also go through troubled periods, especially if one of you tries to manage the affairs of the other without permission. If you cultivate your intuitive ability to read each other's feelings, and are respectful of each other, you will get along very nicely.

1 WATER STAR WITH 2 EARTH STAR

Because 1 Water Star and 2 Earth Star are in conflict, their interaction is challenging, especially to 1 Water Star. Since it takes a relatively long time for 2 Earth to develop trust, 2 Earth will make 1 Water feel insecure. Then, as 2 Earth needs emotional support, 1 Water will feel stifled. Looking at this combination the other way around, 2 Earth will grow suspicious about the mercurial behavior of 1 Water. Try not to exhaust each other.

1 WATER STAR WITH 3 WOOD STAR

Because 1 Water Star supports 3 Wood Star, you can develop a friendly and productive relationship quite easily. 1 Water, being resourceful and subtle, can bring valuable insights and useful suggestions to 3 Wood, while 3 Wood, having the ability to make decisions and plan effective strategies, can bring the inspirations of 1 Water to positive results.

1 WATER STAR WITH 4 WOOD STAR

Because 1 Water Star supports 4 Wood Star, you can have an intellectually rich relationship. While neither one of you is a strong decision maker, you can develop a lot of interesting ideas together, some of which will definitely come to fruition.

1 WATER STAR WITH 5 EARTH STAR

Because 1 Water Star and 5 Earth Star are in conflict, your relationship is a challenge. 5 Earth will ultimately dominate 1 Water and cause 1 Water to feel hemmed in and threatened. Conversely, as 1 Water tries to reassert himself or herself, 5 Earth will grow suspicious. It is healthiest for both of you to establish and respect mutually agreeable boundaries.

1 WATER STAR WITH 6 METAL STAR

Because 1 Water Star is supported by 6 Metal Star, your relationship is friendly and productive. Although 6 Metal can be dominant and critical, 1 Water finds it easy to get along with 6 Metal. Conversely, 6 Metal is naturally supportive of 1 Water and values 1 Water's insightfulness.

1 WATER STAR WITH 7 METAL STAR

Because 1 Water Star is supported by 7 Metal Star, your relationship is both lively and agreeable. You can communicate easily and subtly with each other and can find many interesting business possibilities to bring you both to success.

1 WATER STAR AND 8 EARTH STAR

Because 1 Water Star and 8 Earth Star are in conflict, your relationship is a challenge. 8 Earth can easily block the free-flowing energy of 1 Water. 1 Water will grow to feel insecure and at a disadvantage. Because you tend not to trust each other, it would be wise for both of you to establish and respect mutually agreeable boundaries.

1 WATER STAR AND 9 FIRE STAR

Because 1 Water Star and 9 Fire Star are mutually attractive, it is your way to find harmony together. 1 Water and 9 Fire are opposite and complementary. The success of your relationship depends on finding your common goal. If you do not work toward this, your opposite natures will tend to pull you apart.

2 EARTH STAR AND 2 EARTH STAR

Because your stars are the same, you share characteristics. On the one hand, you are both conservative and caring, and will grow to depend on each other. On the other hand, since neither of you is particularly flexible, you may find it difficult to adjust to each other's individual needs. Notwithstanding, your sincerity toward each other will bring you successfully through whatever difficulties you might experience together.

2 EARTH STAR AND 3 WOOD STAR

Because 2 Earth Star and 3 Wood Star are in conflict, your relationship is a challenge. 2 Earth is cautious and slow going; 3 Wood is decisive and eager to move forward. 2 Earth could judge 3 Wood to be foolhardy; 3 Wood could judge 2 Earth to be a killjoy. 3 Wood needs to exercise patience in order to get along with 2 Earth; 2 Earth needs to take courage in order to get along with 3 Wood. What 2 Earth and 3 Wood share is sensitivity. Learn to care for each other's well-being.

2 EARTH STAR AND 4 WOOD STAR

Because 2 Earth Star and 4 Wood Star are in conflict, your relationship is fraught with difficulties. The two of you can irritate each other. 2 Earth is hesitant and doubtful; 4 Wood is restless and changeable. 4 Wood will criticize 2 Earth for being too limited; 2 Earth will criticize 4 Wood for being too confusing. Although both 2 Earth and 4 Wood are gentle by nature, it is very difficult for them to adapt to each other. Your relationship will require you to make an effort to respect each other.

2 EARTH STAR AND 5 EARTH STAR

Because 2 Earth Star and 5 Earth Star are mutually cooperative, you can be of great benefit to each other. 2 Earth is gentle and trustworthy, and needs to depend on and be helpful to others. 5 Earth is inwardly strong and willingly takes on great responsibilities. 2 Earth and 5 Earth inspire trust in each other. 2 Earth will look to 5 Earth for reliability, and 5 Earth will look to 2 Earth for assistance. This can be a most productive relationship.

2 EARTH STAR AND 6 METAL STAR

Because 2 Earth Star supports 6 Metal Star, your relationship is friendly and productive. 2 Earth nourishes and fosters the powerful leadership abilities of 6 Metal; 6 Metal is loyal and considerate of 2 Earth.

2 EARTH STAR AND 7 METAL STAR

Because 2 Earth Star supports 7 Metal Star, your relationship is friendly and productive. 2 Earth is loyal; 7 Metal is skillful and diplomatic. 7 Metal can rely on 2 Earth for help when needed. 2 Earth will find many rewards in working for 7 Metal.

2 EARTH STAR AND 8 EARTH STAR

Because 2 Earth Star and 8 Earth Star are mutually attractive, it is easy for you to seek a balanced and mutually agreeable course together. 2 Earth's ability to understand and assist 8 Earth allows 8 Earth to trust 2 Earth. Your combined forces will allow you to be positively productive together.

2 EARTH STAR AND 9 FIRE STAR

Because 2 Earth Star is supported by 9 Fire Star, your relationship is friendly and productive. 2 Earth has the ability to produce and complete the creative ideas of 9 Fire; 9 Fire gives encouragement and creative stimulation to 2 Earth.

3 WOOD STAR AND 3 WOOD STAR

Because your stars are the same, you share the same characteristics. This can work for and against you. On the one hand, both of you are optimistic and aspiring. On the other hand, you both can be impatient and short-tempered when you don't agree. Notwithstanding, where you do agree, you can make plans together easily and move forward at the same speed.

3 WOOD STAR AND 4 WOOD STAR

Because 3 Wood Star and 4 Wood Star are mutually cooperative, it is generally easy for you to get along. While both of you are kindhearted, optimistic, and willing to understand each other, you can also get into an occasional spat as a result of your shared impatience. Nonetheless, the clarity and decisive impulse of 3 Wood can bring the energy and imagination of 4 Wood into brilliant focus, while the many-sidedness of 4 Wood acts as a catalyst for the creative thinking of 3 Wood. Communication between you can be richly rewarding.

3 WOOD STAR AND 5 EARTH STAR

Because 3 Wood Star and 5 Earth Star are in conflict, it may be difficult for you to understand each other. 3 Wood acts spontaneously and decisively; 5 Earth sets up boundaries and needs to be in control. The results of this disparity can be frustrating for both of you unless 3 Wood learns self-restraint and 5 Earth learns flexibility and compassion.

3 WOOD STAR AND 6 METAL STAR

Because 3 Wood Star and 6 Metal Star are in conflict, your relationship is a challenge. 3 Wood will tend to become impatient with, and exhausted by, the authoritative and critical attitudes of 6 Metal, while 6 Metal will find it difficult to put up with the impulsive nature of 3 Wood. You might work effectively toward a common goal, however, when 3 Wood is willing to conform to, or agree with, the dictates of 6 Metal.

3 WOOD STAR AND 7 METAL STAR

Because 3 Wood Star and 7 Metal Star are mutually attractive, you seek a mutually agreeable way together. Both of you are sensitive and can think, communicate, and act with ease. You will be richly productive together when you have a common goal.

3 WOOD STAR AND 8 EARTH STAR

Because 3 Wood Star and 8 Earth Star are in conflict, your relationship is a challenge. 8 Earth will tend to resist the spontaneous approach of 3 Wood, while 3 Wood will tend to become frustrated by 8 Earth's resistance. Unless you work on your relationship, it will be difficult for you to understand each other.

3 WOOD STAR AND 9 FIRE STAR

Because 3 Wood Star supports 9 Fire Star, your relationship is a highly creative one. While you are both expansive, active, far seeing, and imaginative, you are also volatile and capable of quarreling with each other. Notwithstanding, since you enjoy working together, the results can be innovative and brilliant.

4 WOOD STAR AND 4 WOOD STAR

Because your stars are the same, you share characteristics. You both are easygoing and imaginative, but because neither of you finds it easy to be decisive, you could drift apart. Nevertheless, you can generate many useful ideas and share your insights with each other. You both communicate easily.

4 WOOD STAR AND 5 EARTH STAR

Because 4 Wood Star and 5 Earth Star are in conflict, your relationship tends to be discordant. 5 Earth will seek to control 4 Wood, while 4 Wood will worry 5 Earth by seeing through and evading 5 Earth's demands. Eventually 4 Wood will become distressed by the rigidity of 5 Earth as 5 Earth puts up more and more barriers. Unless you work to understand your own idiosyncrasies and agree to respect each other, you will have discord.

4 WOOD STAR AND 6 METAL STAR

Because 4 Wood Star and 6 Metal Star are mutually attractive, you need to find a mutually agreeable way. This may not be so easy, since your natures are quite opposite. 4 Wood is flexible and emotionally sensitive; 6 Metal is inflexible and idealistic. Where you find a common purpose, you will work well together. However, 6 Metal will eventually gain control over 4 Wood.

4 WOOD STAR AND 7 METAL STAR

Because 4 Wood Star and 7 Metal Star are in conflict, your relationship could be tricky. Both of you are good communicators, and are sociable and accommodating, but 4 Wood acts out of emotional sensitivity, while 7 Metal is calculating and shrewd. Eventually 4 Wood could question the sincerity of 7 Metal, and 7 Metal could question the motives of 4 Wood. You can be productive together when you share a common goal. But if 7 Metal tries to control 4 Wood too much, 4 Wood will escape.

4 WOOD STAR AND 8 EARTH STAR

Because 4 Wood Star and 8 Earth Star are in conflict, your relationship is a challenge. 4 Wood is flexible and curious, while 8 Earth is unbending and resistant.

Because of your differences you can exhaust each other. Unless you make a conscious effort to understand and adjust to each other, it will be difficult for you to cooperate.

4 WOOD STAR AND 9 FIRE STAR

Because 4 Wood Star supports 9 Fire Star, yours is a harmonious and productive relationship. 4 Wood is many-sided and inventive, while 9 Fire is insightful and imaginative. It will be easy for you to work together, especially when 9 Fire takes the lead.

5 EARTH STAR AND 5 EARTH STAR

Because your stars are the same and are mutually attractive, it is essential for you to seek a way that works equally well for both of you. You are both stubborn, unyielding, and prone to being suspicious and argumentative. However, where you find a common cause, you can cooperate successfully. Be careful to negotiate your boundaries.

5 EARTH STAR AND 6 METAL STAR

Because 5 Earth Star supports 6 Metal Star, your relationship is friendly and mutually advantageous. Although both of you are strong willed and proud, you naturally tend to respect each other. You could become strong political allies.

5 EARTH STAR AND 7 METAL STAR

Because 5 Earth Star supports 7 Metal Star, you can work well together. If 7 Metal believes in 5 Earth's aims, 7 Metal can help 5 Earth by applying his or her refined diplomatic and social abilities to 5 Earth's advantage. 5 Earth tends to admire the adaptability and shrewdness of 7 Metal.

5 EARTH STAR AND 8 EARTH STAR

Because 5 Earth Star and 8 Earth Star are mutually cooperative, you can work well together once you overcome your suspicions of each other. Even though both of you are cautious, independent, and willful, 5 Earth will eventually come to value

8 Earth's farsightedness, and 8 Earth will come to value 5 Earth's strength and supportiveness.

5 EARTH STAR AND 9 FIRE STAR

Because 9 Fire Star supports 5 Earth Star, you can relate to each other easily. While 9 Fire will encourage the impulsive side of 5 Earth's nature, 5 Earth will stabilize 9 Fire. You can become strong creative and political partners.

6 METAL STAR AND 6 METAL STAR

Because your stars are the same, you share characteristics. Both of you are idealistic, critical, and unyielding. If you do not hold the same ideals or views, you could clash and offend each other. Your relationship requires mutual respect.

6 METAL STAR AND 7 METAL STAR

Because 6 Metal Star and 7 Metal Star are mutually cooperative, you can communicate with each other easily. You need to be careful not to offend each other, however. The blunt and often caustic manner of 6 Metal can alarm 7 Metal, while the calculated and biting remarks of 7 Metal can arouse the contempt of 6 Metal. Mutual respect is the watchword for your relationship.

6 METAL STAR AND 8 EARTH STAR

Because 6 Metal Star is supported by 8 Earth Star, your relationship can be peaceful and productive. Both of you are high-minded and visionary. You can communicate easily with each other. The organizational abilities of 6 Metal complement 8 Earth's abilities to build.

6 METAL STAR AND 9 FIRE STAR

Because 6 Metal Star and 9 Fire Star are in conflict, you may find it difficult to agree with each other. The energy of 6 Metal is cool and orderly, while 9 Fire is hot and volatile. 6 Metal will find it difficult to tolerate the volatility and pride of 9 Fire. 9 Fire will be challenged by 6 Metal's need to be in control. Your relationship requires you to observe decorum and develop mutual respect.

7 METAL STAR AND 7 METAL STAR

Because your stars are the same, you share characteristics. You both are diplomatic and astute, so you may not gain each other's trust too readily. However, when you agree to cooperate, you work effectively and powerfully together.

7 METAL STAR AND 8 EARTH STAR

Because 7 Metal Star is supported by 8 Earth Star, your relationship is productive and rewarding. 8 Earth will admire the subtlety and accommodating flexibility of 7 Metal, while 7 Metal will admire the adventurousness and stubborn determination of 8 Earth.

7 METAL STAR AND 9 FIRE STAR

Because 7 Metal Star and 9 Fire Star are in conflict, your relationship can become problematic. Although you are both artistic and stylish, and can share interests, your natures are very different. 7 Metal is calculating and subtle; 9 Fire is volatile and outspoken. You will tend to clash with each other unless you maintain mutual respect.

8 EARTH STAR AND 8 EARTH STAR

Because your stars are the same, you share characteristics. You both are adventurous and visionary. You are also excellent at building and planning. However, because both of you are self-centered and willful, you can grow suspicious of each other. If you respect each other, you can be very productive together.

8 EARTH STAR AND 9 FIRE STAR

Because 8 Earth Star is supported by 9 Fire Star, your relationship can be productive and rewarding. Both of you are visionary and adventurous. When 8 Earth knows the value of 9 Fire's creative ideas, she will turn them to profit.

9 FIRE STAR AND 9 FIRE STAR

Because your stars are the same, you share characteristics. You are both highly active and expansive. You can collaborate successfully on creative projects while enjoying each other's fiery imagination and wit. However, be careful not to let your pride get in your way; you could ruin your relationship by quarreling.

EXERCISE

Compare your birth star, month star, and tendency star with the birth stars, month stars, and tendency stars of various members of your family, friends, and colleagues at work. Be careful to compare your birth star only with their birth stars, your month star only with their month stars, and your tendency star only with their tendency stars. Also, remember that the birth star signifies basic personality, the month star signifies mental characteristics, and the tendency star signifies outlook on life.

chapter 6

FORECASTING

Nine star astrology provides an interesting and simple method for predicting the changing conditions in your life on a yearly and even monthly basis. The changes are cyclical, and they are timed in accordance with the Chinese solar calendar. Although Chinese and Japanese astrologers usually combine the nine star method of forecasting with other astrological methods, it can be used alone. I find the yearly forecasts in nine star astrology more significant and noteworthy than the monthly forecasts. However, the monthly forecasts are often surprisingly meaningful as well.

If you are planning to make an important strategic move in your career, find out the best time by reading first the forecast for the year, then the paragraph for each month of the year. The months in which both the year and the month forecasts reveal the greatest probabilities for success are the best months to plan your moves.

In this chapter you will find the forecasts for your business future arranged in seventy-two paragraphs. Use the following four tables to find your own year and month forecasts. Directions follow the tables.

UNIVERSAL YEAR STARS

Year	Star	Year	Star
1998	2	2009	9
1999	1	2010	8
2000	9	2011	7
2001	8	2012	6
2002	7	2013	5
2003	6	2014	4
2004	5	2015	3
2005	4	2016	2
2006	3	2017	1
2007	2	2018	9
2008	1	2019	8
		2020	7

CHINESE SOLAR MONTHS

Chinese Month	Equivalent Western Dates
1	February 4th through March 4th
2	March 5th through April 4th
3	April 5th through May 4th
4	May 5th through June 5th
5	June 6th through July 6th
6	July 7th through August 6th
7	August 7th through September 6th
8	September 7th through October 7th
9	October 8th through November 6th
10	November 7th through December 6th
11	December 7th through January 4th
12	January 5th through February 3rd

UNIVERSAL MONTH STARS

Chinese Month	1	2	3	4	5	6	7	8	9	10	11	12
Year Star 1,4,7	8	7	6	5	4	3	2	1	9	8	7	6
3,6,9	5	4	3	2	1	9	8	7	6	5	4	3
2,5,8	2	1	9	8	7	6	5	4	3	2	1	9

INDEX OF YEAR AND MONTH FORECASTS

In the Index of Year and Month Forecasts, the birth stars are listed in numerical order, except that 5 is not listed. If you are a man born under 5 Earth Star, use birth star 2 to find your forecasts. If you are a woman born under 5 Earth Star, use birth star 8 to find your forecasts.

Universal Year or Month Star	1	2	3	4	5	6	7	8	9
Your Birth Star 1	5	4	3	2	1	9	8	7	6
2	15	14	13	12	11	10	18	17	16
3	25	24	23	22	21	20	19	27	26
4	35	34	33	32	31	30	29	28	36
6	37	45	44	43	42	41	40	39	38
7	47	46	54	53	52	51	50	49	48
8	57	56	55	63	62	61	60	59	58
9	67	66	65	64	72	71	70	69	68

FINDING YOUR YEAR FORECAST

To learn your forecast for a particular year in the future, first find the star number of the year you want to read about in the universal year stars table. Next, go to the Index of Year and Month Forecasts. Using your birth star number in the left column and the star number for the year in question in the top row, find the appropriate paragraph number where the horizontal and vertical lines intersect.

For example, if your birth star is 1 Water Star and you want to read your forecast for 1998, a 2 Earth Star year, you will want to read paragraph 4. If your birth star is 2 Earth Star and you want to read your forecast for 1998, you will want to read paragraph 14. If your birth star is 3 Wood Star and you want to read your forecast for the year 2001, an 8 Earth Star year, you will want to read paragraph 27.

Remember that the Chinese solar year begins on February 4th. This means that your year forecasts start on each February 4th, not on January 1st, as in the Western calendar.

FINDING YOUR MONTH FORECAST

- In the universal year stars table, find the star number of the year in which you want a month forecast.
- In the table of Chinese solar months, find the Chinese month according to the equivalent Western dates. For instance, the period from February 4th through March 4th is the first Chinese month; the period from March 5th through April 4th is the second Chinese month, and so on.
- Having found the Chinese month, go to the universal month stars table. Where the horizontal line extending from the year star number and the vertical line extending from the Chinese month meet, you will find the universal month star number.

For example, suppose you want to find the month star number for the period February 4th through March 4th of the year 1999. First you will see in the universal year stars table that 1999 is a 1 Water Star year. Next you will see in the table of Chinese solar months that February 4th begins the first Chinese month. Then, referring to the universal month stars table, you will see that the first Chinese month of a year whose star number is 1 has 8 as its month star number. For another example, let's say you want to find the month star number for the period May 5th through June 5th of the year 2002. You will see in the universal year stars table that the year 2002 has the star number 7. Next you will see in the table of Chinese solar months that May 5th begins the fourth Chinese month. Then, referring to the universal month stars table, you will see that the fourth Chinese month of a year whose star number is 7 has 5 as its month star number.

- After you have found the correct month star number, refer to the Index of Year and Month Forecasts. Using your birth star number and the appropriate month star number, you will find the correct paragraph number to read the same way you found your year forecast.

For example, if your birth star number is 1 (1 Water Star) and the star number for the Chinese month in question is 1, you will want to read paragraph 5. If your birth star number is 2 (2 Earth Star) and the star number for the Chinese month in question is 1, you will want to read paragraph 15.

Remember, year forecasts carry more weight than month forecasts. When reading your month forecasts, try to understand them in the context of your year forecast. With each forecast I give a quotation from the *Analects* of Confucius. Use these as guides for positive action, as well as for avoiding any of the negative possibilities indicated. You will notice a special paragraph at the end of each forecast dealing with favorable and unfavorable directions for moving either your office or your home during the forecast period. Unless the move is short term, the indications for a move made under a year forecast are far more significant than those made under a month forecast.

THE FORECASTS

1   Try to be patient throughout this emotionally stressful period, when you may be under a great deal of pressure. Friends and allies could be out of reach when you need them. This is a difficult time for business activities in general, and for new ventures or projects in particular. Keep your opinions to yourself; try to avoid arguments and gossip. Your confidences can be betrayed. Misunderstandings could lead to demotion or job loss. Be impeccable about your commitments. "The reason why the ancients did not readily give utterance to their words was that they feared lest their actions should not come up to them" (*Analects* IV:22).

If you plan to move during this period, avoid moving directly north or south. All other directions are favorable.

2   With patience and perseverance, your affairs will turn out well throughout

this period. It is a time of gradual change for the better. Be conservative with money. Large-scale investments may prove troublesome. Take your time while working out your future plans and developing new business relationships. Be thorough and circumspect in your dealings. This is not the best time to plunge into business ventures; it is better to wait and watch. Inept leadership will result in failure. Be mindful of your reputation. "If the superior man loves propriety, the people will not dare to be irreverent. If he loves righteousness, the people will not dare not to follow his example. If he loves good faith, the people will not dare not to be sincere" (*Analects* XIII:4).

If you plan to move during this period, avoid moving northeast, southeast, southwest, or northwest. All other directions are favorable.

3   Master yourself before becoming concerned with mastering others. You are in a period of rapid advancement that can lead to great success or failure, depending on actions rooted in the past. This period favors undoing past errors, making decisions, taking initiative, and entering new territory. Avoid fighting. Your anger and cunning will only bring serious repercussions. Let go of any resentment you are harboring. "Po-i and Shu-chi never paid any mind to the past wrongs of others, for which reason the others almost never bore a grudge against them" (*Analects* V:22).

If you plan to move during this period, avoid moving east or west. All other directions are favorable.

4   When you show generosity of spirit, the obstacles to your success will give way. You are in a period when positive activities begun in the past will pay off. This is a favorable time for all business activities and travel. You will find other people friendly and cooperative. You can confidently look forward to a promotion and to financial gains now. Be flexible and adaptable to the changing conditions of the time. "If a prince is able to govern his realm with courtesy, what trouble will he have? If he cannot govern it with courtesy, what good will the rules of proper conduct do him?" (*Analects* IV:13).

If you plan to move during this period, avoid moving northeast, southeast, southwest, or northwest. All other directions are favorable.

5   Be patient and careful. This period marks a turning point in your affairs. Matters that are rooted in the past will come to a head for good or ill, while whatever you start now will take on great meaning for your future. Be careful in your dealings with others. Misunderstandings can put you at a critical disadvantage, and quarrels can cause your downfall. Avoid putting your hopes in questionable schemes and relying on the help of unreliable people. "Fan Chih asked about benevolence. The master said, 'It is to love all men.' He asked about knowledge. The master said, 'Employ the upright and put aside all the crooked; in this way the crooked will be made to be upright'" (*Analects* XII:22).

This is not a good period to move unless it is to a distant location. If you do plan to move, however, avoid moving north or south. All other directions are permitted.

6   Take full advantage of your opportunities. You are in a fortunate period that favors moving up in rank, expanding business activities, traveling, taking on greater responsibilities, making investments, obtaining funds, and improving relations with your superiors. However, considering your natural bent to pursue your aims forcefully, be careful not to arouse the hostility of others. When difficulties arise, be adaptable. Your willingness to be helpful will ensure your progress and lead to your success. Avoid making enemies. "If a man takes no thought about what is distant, he will eventually find sorrow near at hand" (*Analects* XV:11).

If you plan to move during this period, avoid moving north, southeast, south, or northwest. All other directions are favorable.

7   Be levelheaded. You are in a period when overexpansion, presumptuous anticipation of big profits, or overspending could spell big disappointments. Nonetheless, the time favors financial growth and positive dealings with others. When you find your plans in abeyance, take advantage of the time by improving your skills and increasing your knowledge. If out of impatience you try to force your way, you will only cause others to lose confidence in you, and you may have to abandon a potentially fortunate opportunity.

Reflect on your actions. "The progress of the superior man is upwards; the progress of the mean man is downwards" (*Analects* XIV:24).

If you plan to move during this period, avoid moving northeast, east, southwest, or west. All other directions are favorable.

Be watchful and patient. You are in a transitional period that may call for some reforms. Some of your business affairs may come to an end or change direction, while other activities that have been dormant may come back to life. Communication with others is critical; thus, be careful of your words. Do not count too much on the cooperation of others, or on being promoted. Restrain yourself, and avoid exerting undue pressure on others. Show them respect. Attempting to force your way will meet with resistance and arouse enmity. "The superior man holds virtue to be of the highest importance. A man in a high position, having courage without virtue, will be tempted to commit insubordination; one of the lower people, having courage without virtue, will be tempted to commit robbery" (*Analects* XVII:23).

If you plan to move during this period, avoid moving east, southwest, west, or northwest. All other directions are favorable.

9 Be willing to make adjustments. This is a time of extremes. Beware of misplaced confidence. You could be taken by surprise. Matters heretofore kept secret from you will come to light. Your secrets could become public knowledge as well. If your business dealings have been shady, you may be exposed. At worst, you may run the risk of a lawsuit, demotion, or job loss. If your track record has been good, however, a promotion may be in store for you. You might also receive a surprise bonus, or if you are an artist, writer, or scientist, you may gain public recognition. Documents, signatures, meetings, and partings of the way count significantly in this period. When dealing with others, look beyond the surface. "The superior man does not promote a man simply on account of his words, nor does he put aside good words because of the man" (*Analects* XV:22).

If you plan to move during this period, avoid moving north, south, southwest, or northwest. All other directions are favorable.

10 Be calm and patient through this emotionally stressful period. You are likely to come under considerable pressure. Unless you are employed as a researcher, this could be a difficult time at work, especially if you are new at your job. Stick to routines, and conserve your strength and finances; progress will be slow, maybe difficult. Be careful about placing your trust and confidence in others. Misunderstandings and quarrels can easily result in a demotion or job loss. If you remain steadfast and calm, however, you will come through this period with flying colors. Cultivate your trustworthiness. "I do not know how an untrustworthy man is to get on. How can a carriage be made to go without yoking the horses?" (*Analects* II:22).

   If you plan to move during this period, avoid moving north, southeast, south, or northwest. All other directions are favorable.

11 With hard work all will turn out well during this period. It is a time for slow and steady progress. Take deliberate and well-thought-out steps, use your money conservatively, and take your time to work out your plans, improve your relationships, and develop new business contacts. Be flexible, and avoid quarreling, because conflicts can easily result in an eventual demotion or job loss. Cultivate tolerance, a liberal view, and humanity. "It is only the truly virtuous man who can love or hate others" (*Analects* IV:3).

   If you plan to move during this period, avoid moving northeast or southwest. All other directions are favorable.

12 Expect the unexpected. Seize your opportunities for success. You are in a period of rapid development that can bring you great success or failure. Pay attention to details. Your positive efforts will pay off. You can be promoted or make surprising gains. This is a time for making decisions, taking initiative, and entering new territory. If you want to avoid potential trouble, do not boast about your plans and political connections. "The superior man is slow to speak and serious in his conduct" (*Analects* V:24).

   If you plan to move during this period, avoid moving east, southeast, west, or northwest. All other directions are favorable.

13   Broaden your outlook. Positive activities begun in the past will come to fruition. Good news is on the way. This is an auspicious time for all business activities, social activities, and travel. Other people will be helpful and friendly to you. Go forward, confident of promotion and financial gains. There's no need to rush, however. Take your time. "Do not desire to do things quickly; do not look at small advantages. Doing things too quickly prevents their being done thoroughly. Looking at small advantages prevents great things from being accomplished" (*Analects* XIII:17).

   If you plan to move during this period, avoid moving east, southeast, west, or northwest. All other directions are favorable.

14   Be patient and cautious. This period marks a critical turning point in your affairs, in which activities begun in the past will come to a head for good or ill. Whatever you begin in this period will also take on great meaning in the future. Be especially careful in your dealings with others. Misunderstandings will put you at a serious disadvantage, while cooperation will ensure your success. You could be promoted or otherwise rewarded for your good efforts. Weigh your conduct against the four things that Confucius taught: "erudition, ethics, devotion, and truthfulness" (*Analects* VIII:24).

   This is not a good period to move unless it is to a distant location. If you do plan to move, however, avoid moving northeast or southwest. All other directions are permitted.

15   Take advantage of your opportunities. You are in a fortunate period that favors moving up in rank, expanding business activities, taking on greater responsibilities, making investments, obtaining funds, traveling, attending business meetings, and improving relations with your superiors. Be careful, however, not to force your way. If you provoke the hostility of others, you may meet with censure, eventual demotion, or even job loss. Be mindful of your proper limits. "The superior man thinks of virtue; the small man thinks of comfort. The superior man thinks of the sanctions of the law; the small man thinks of the favors he may receive" (*Analects* IV:11).

If you plan to move during this period, avoid moving north, southeast, south, or northwest. All other directions are favorable.

16 Be levelheaded. You are in a period when overexpansion, overoptimism, overspending, or presumptuous anticipation of windfalls and big profits could spell big disappointments. Nonetheless, this period favors financial growth and productive dealings with others. If you are certain of your goals, you will make definite progress. You also may receive a promotion. Be clear and honest about negotiating your needs. Partnership agreements could fall through at the last minute unless everything is clearly spelled out and understood. Be alert to possible deceptions. "He who does not anticipate deceptions or lies, yet apprehends them readily when they occur—is he not a man of superior worth?" (*Analects* XIV:33).

If you plan to move during this period, avoid moving north, east, south, or west. All other directions are favorable.

17 Be watchful. You are in a transitional period that calls for crucial decisions and possible corrections. Some of your business activities may come to an end or take on a new direction, while other activities or interests that have been dormant may come back to life. If you follow a middle course and are cooperative with others, you will be successful and may be promoted or rewarded. Exerting undue pressure on others, however, will only bring resistance. Exercise self-restraint. "The master fished with a pole, but did not use a net. He shot, but not at birds that were nesting" (*Analects* VII:26).

If you plan to move during this period, avoid moving northeast or southwest. All other directions are favorable.

18 Be modest and trustworthy. Matters heretofore kept secret from you will come to light. Your secrets could become public knowledge as well. If your past business dealings were illegal, you could be exposed and have to suffer the consequences. On the other hand, you could make surprisingly rapid progress, win the support of your colleagues and superiors, be promoted, or receive a surprise bonus, or if you are an artist, writer, or scientist, you could

gain public recognition. Documents, signatures, meetings, and partings of the way count significantly in this period. Avoid disputes. "The superior man is modest in his speech, but excels in his actions" (*Analects* XIV:29).

If you plan to move during this period, avoid moving north, east, south, or west. All other directions are favorable.

19   You are likely to come under considerable pressure during this period. Be tolerant and quiet to minimize the possibilities of emotional stress. This is not an easy time for your ventures, especially those that are just beginning. Progress may be uncertain. Stick to routines, be careful with your money, and avoid quarrels. Misunderstandings and fighting could lead eventually to your demotion or job loss. When encountering difficulties, just sit back and wait for conditions to improve. Avoid confiding in the wrong people. "There are three friendships which are advantageous, and three which are injurious. Friendships with the honest, the sincere, and the observant are advantageous. Friendships with the dishonest, the obsequious, and the glib-tongued are injurious" (*Analects* XVI:4).

If you plan to move during this period, avoid moving north, east, south, or west. All other directions are favorable.

20   Persevere. This period favors slow, steady progress. It is a time to be conservative with money, cultivate new business relations, and patiently make plans for the future. Be cautious if you take the lead in business ventures now. Avoid making claims and commitments that you will not be able to keep. Doing so for the sake of having your way will result in misfortune, while modesty and self-restraint will ensure the ultimate success of your plans. Practice self-discipline. "He who requires much from himself and little from others will keep himself from being the object of resentment" (*Analects* XV:14).

If you plan to move during this period, avoid moving northeast, southeast, southwest, or northwest. All other directions are favorable.

21   Stay focused. You are in a period of rapid development that will bring you success or failure, depending on your attitude. Be positive and optimistic. Pay

attention to details, and be open to surprising turns of events. This period favors making decisions, taking initiative, and entering new territory. You could make some surprising gains. Be careful not to become headstrong. Be alert. Forcing your way against better judgment will bring losses. Reflect on your pride. "In letters I am perhaps equal to other men, but the character of the superior man, carrying out what he professes, is what I have not yet attained to" (*Analects* VII:32).

If you plan to move during this period, avoid moving east or west. All other directions are favorable.

22 Broaden your horizons. You are in a period when positive activities begun in the past will bear fruit. This is an auspicious time for all business activities, meetings, negotiations, and travel. Good news is on the way. Others will be cooperative. Go forward confident of a promotion and financial gains. You might gain through seemingly unfortunate circumstances. Reflect on your ability to be open and sincere with others. "The way of the superior man is threefold. Honest, he is free from anxiety; wise, he is free from confusion; courageous, he is free from fear" (*Analects* XIV:30).

If you plan to move during this period, avoid moving southeast or north-west. All other directions are favorable.

23 Be cautious and patient. You are in a period that will mark a critical turning point in your affairs. Your past activities will come to a head for good or ill, while whatever you start now will loom in importance in the future. Carefully consider what it is that you wish to accomplish, and be wide awake in your dealings with other people. Avoid impulsive actions. Fooling yourself and misreading others will put you at a critical disadvantage. Quarreling can result in your defeat. Consider how you can be of help to others; in this way you will be favored by those who are in a position to help you. Stay focused on your goals, fulfill your commitments, and be tolerant. "Empty words con-found virtue. Want of forbearance in small matters confounds great plans" (*Analects* XV:26).

This is not a good period to move unless it is to a distant location. If you do plan to move, however, avoid moving east or west. All other directions are permitted.

24 Take advantage of your opportunities. You are in a fortunate period that favors moving up in rank, expanding your business activities, taking on greater responsibilities, making investments, obtaining funds, traveling, meeting new people, attending business meetings, and improving relations with your superiors. Be careful not to step on other people's toes. With your current bent to pursue your aims more forcefully than you normally do, you could easily incite the enmity of others. Your integrity will be tested. Reflect on your motives. "He who acts with a constant view to his own advantage will be much murmured against" (*Analects* IV:12).

If you plan to move during this period, avoid moving northeast, southeast, southwest, or northwest. All other directions are favorable.

25 Be practical. You are in a period when overexpansion, overoptimism, overspending, or presumptuous expectation of windfalls and big profits could spell big disappointments. Nonetheless, this period favors financial growth through positive dealings with others. Be careful when communicating with others. Pay attention to details to avoid misunderstandings. Contracts and partnership agreements could fall through at the last minute unless everything is clearly spelled out and understood. If you maintain high goals and are constructive in your actions, you will be helped by your superiors and could be promoted. Consider how you pursue your goals. "There are five things that constitute perfect virtue. They are seriousness, generosity, sincerity, earnestness, and kindness. If you are serious, you will not be treated with disrespect. If you are generous, you will win all. If you are earnest, you will accomplish much. If you are kind, you will be able to employ the services of others" (*Analects* XVII:6).

If you plan to move during this period, avoid moving north, east, south, or west. All other directions are favorable.

26 Be down-to-earth and watchful. You are in a transitional period that may call

for reorganization. Some of your business activities could come to an end or take on a new direction, while other activities that have been lying dormant may show new life. Communication with others is critical and may be difficult. Be careful not to pressure others. Attempting to force your way will only result in resistance. On the other hand, considering how you might be of help to others will win their favor and lead to your eventual promotion. Try to be realistic. "The master never spoke about extraordinary things, feats of strength, chaos, and spiritual entities" (*Analects* VII:20).

If you plan to move during this period, avoid moving north, northeast, south, or southwest. All other directions are favorable.

27 Strive to turn adverse conditions to your advantage. Be prepared for surprises. You are in a period when your secrets could become public knowledge. If your past business dealings have been illegal, you may be exposed and have to suffer the consequences. On the other hand, this could be a highly creative time in which you make rapid progress, win the support of your colleagues and superiors, are promoted, or receive a surprise bonus, or if you are an artist, writer, or scientist, you may gain public recognition. Documents, signatures, meetings, and partings of the way count significantly in this period. When relating to others, maintain equilibrium. "Can there be love which does not lead to strictness with its object? Can there be loyalty which does not lead to the instruction of its object?" (*Analects* XIV:8).

If you plan to move during this period, avoid moving north, northeast, south, or southwest. All other directions are favorable.

28 Be flexible and tolerant, because you are likely to come under considerable pressure during this uncertain period. It will not be an easy time for your enterprises and business relationships, especially those that are new. Proceed cautiously, stick to routines as much as possible, and above all avoid arguments. Quarrels could eventually lead to your demotion or job loss. On the other hand, cultivating a friendly and cooperative attitude will serve to improve your reputation and eventually lead to your promotion and greater prosperity. Reflect on your conduct. "When you go abroad, behave to every-

one as if you were receiving a great guest; employ others as if you were assisting at a great sacrifice; not to do to others as you would not wish done to yourself" (*Analects* XII:2).

If you plan to move during this period, avoid moving north, northeast, south, or southwest. All other directions are favorable.

29 Pay attention to details. You are now in a period that favors slow, steady progress. Be conservative when investing your money, cultivate new business contacts, and patiently make plans for the future. Do not take the lead in ambitious ventures. Forcing your way while making empty promises may result in loss. Do not overestimate your strength. Consideration of the views of others, however, will win their support and lead to the ultimate success of your plans. Be thorough in all you do and deliberate in your actions. "The cautious seldom err" (*Analects* IV:23).

If you are planning to move during this period, avoid moving east, southwest, west, or northwest. All other directions are favorable.

30 Be bold. You are in a period of rapid development that demands concentration. Pay attention to details, and be open to surprises. This period favors making decisions, taking initiative, and entering new territory. You could make some surprising gains. Creative activities will flourish. Vacillation and inconsistency, however, will lead to misfortune. Be self-confident and consistent. "The state may lose its military commander, but a man cannot lose his will" (*Analects* IX:25).

If you plan to move during this period, avoid moving east, southeast, west, or northwest. All other directions are favorable.

31 Be decisive. You are in a period when positive activities begun in the past will bear fruit. This is an auspicious time for all business affairs and travel. Progress in general will be rapid and easy. Go forward confident of an eventual promotion and increased prosperity. Honor your commitments. "Let your words be sincere and truthful, and your actions honorable and careful; such conduct will be appreciated in all lands. However, if your words are not sincere and

103

truthful, and your actions are not honorable and careful, how can you expect to be appreciated even in your own neighborhood?" (*Analects* XV:5).

If you plan to move during this period, avoid moving southeast or northwest. All other directions are favorable.

32 Stay centered. You are in a crucial period when matters rooted in the past will come to a climax for good or ill, while whatever actions you take now will bear great consequences for your future. Be wide awake in relating to others. Self-deception and misunderstandings can put you at a critical disadvantage that will result in your downfall. Uproot harmful thoughts, and refrain from harmful actions. "The superior man encourages the admirable qualities of men, and does not encourage their vicious qualities. The mean man does the opposite of this" (*Analects* XII:16).

This is not a good period to move unless it is to a distant location. If you do plan to move, however, avoid moving southeast or northwest. All other directions are permitted.

33 Take advantage of your opportunities. You are in a fortunate period that favors moving up in rank with the help of a superior, expanding your business activities, taking on greater responsibilities, making investments, obtaining funds, traveling, meeting new people, and attending business meetings. You may meet someone of superior character in whom you can place your trust. If your aim is success at any cost without a sense of responsibility, you will incite the hostility of others and jeopardize your standing in the long run. Consider your fortunate position. "He who exercises government by means of his virtue may be compared to the North Star, which keeps its place while all the other stars circle around it" (*Analects* II:1).

If you plan to move during this period, avoid moving east, southeast, west, or northwest. All other directions are favorable.

34 Be realistic. You are in a period when overexpansion and unwarranted expectations of windfalls and big profits could spell big headaches. Nonetheless, this period favors financial growth through intelligent interactions with oth-

ers. Be forthright and honest when communicating. Pay attention to details to avoid misunderstandings. Partnership agreements and contracts could fail unless everything is clearly spelled out and agreed upon. The free and inspired expression of your talents will win the esteem of others and lead to your promotion. Take courage. "Heaven produced virtue in me. What can my enemies do to me?" (*Analects* VII:22).

If you are planning to move during this period, avoid moving northeast, east, southwest, or west. All other directions are favorable.

35   Be self-possessed in the face of possible reversals. You are in a transitional period that may call for extensive reorganization. Some of your business activities may come to an end or take on a new direction, while other activities that have been lying dormant may reemerge. Where you are in a position of responsibility, communication will be difficult. Try to avoid correcting the mistakes of others too harshly. Your intolerance will give you cause for regret. Examine your need for perfection. "How do I dare to think of myself as a sage and man of perfect virtue? It may simply be said of me that I strive tirelessly to become such, and teach others without weariness" (*Analects* VII:33).

If you plan to move during this period, avoid moving north, northeast, south, or southwest. All other directions are favorable.

36   Be alert. You could be taken by surprise. Matters heretofore kept secret from you will come to light. Your secrets may become public knowledge as well. If your past business and financial practices have been unsound, you could become involved in serious conflicts. At worst, you run the risk of demotion, job loss, severed business relationships, or a lawsuit. On the other hand, you could make surprisingly rapid progress, win the support of your colleagues and superiors, be promoted, or receive a surprise bonus, or if you are an artist, writer, or scientist, you may gain public recognition. Documents, signatures, meetings, and partings of the way are particularly significant in this period. Focus unwaveringly on your true goal. "When the year becomes cold, then we know how the pine and the cypress are the last to lose their leaves" (*Analects* IX:27).

If you plan to move during this period, avoid moving south or north. All other directions are favorable.

37 Where you sense danger, retreat and see what develops before making a decision. You need to be tolerant through this uncertain period in order to manage stressful conditions. This period will not be easy for your business activities, especially those that are just beginning. Stick to routines, and avoid entanglements. Misunderstandings and quarrels could lead to your eventual demotion or job loss. On the other hand, seeking the cooperation and friendly support of others now will ensure the eventual success of your aims. Wait calmly for auspicious opportunities to appear. "When the master was unoccupied with business, his manner was easy, and he looked pleased" (*Analects* VII:4).

If you plan to move during this period, avoid moving north or south. All other directions are favorable.

38 Consider implementing new methods. You are now in a period characterized by gradual and positive developments. Be conservative about your financial moves, and take your time to work out plans and develop new business contacts. Beware of flattery and deception. Exercise tact, patience, and caution when taking the lead. The ambitious pursuit of your objectives will arouse enmity and lead to misfortune. Consider the universal good. "If a ruler's words are good, is it not good that no one opposes them? But if the ruler's words are not good, and no one opposes them, is it not fair to say that this is how the state can be ruined?" (*Analects* XIII:15).

If you plan to move during this period, avoid moving north, northeast, south, or southwest. All other directions are favorable.

39 Be fair in your use of power. You are in a period of rapid development that will bring you to either great success or failure. Stay focused, pay attention to details, and be ready to handle surprising developments. This period favors making decisions, taking initiative, and entering new territory. If your projects are well organized, they will flourish and bring surprising gains. If you

have been in an inactive position, your situation will change dramatically. Now is the time to achieve your goals. Exercise your leadership abilities. "Good government exists when those who are near are made happy, and those who are far off are attracted" (*Analects* XIII:16).

If you plan to move during this period, avoid moving northeast, east, southwest, or west. All other directions are favorable.

40   Be innovative. You are in a period when positive activities begun in the past will pay off. This is an auspicious time for all business matters and travel. Good news is on the way. You will find others cooperative and friendly. Go forward confident of your eventual promotion and increased prosperity. Avoid being suspicious of others, because this will cause you unnecessary problems. Seize the moment. "In archery, striking the target is not the principal thing because people's strength is not equal. The moment of release is the principal thing. This is the old way" (*Analects* III:16).

If you plan to move during this period, avoid moving east, southeast, west, or northwest. All other directions are favorable.

41   Retreat from conflict. This period marks a turning point in which your activities begun in the past will come to a head for good or ill, while whatever you start now will take on great meaning for your future. Be careful about how you relate to others. Misunderstandings and quarrels can put you at a critical disadvantage and lead to your downfall. When confronted with difficulties, do not react but wait calmly for conditions to change. Reflect on the ways power can be abused. "To reject people without having instructed them is called cruelty. To demand the fulfillment of their tasks without giving them enough time is called oppression. To lightly issue orders and at the last minute to sharply command their execution is called being a snake in the grass. To be stingy in rewarding others is called playing the part of a mere bureaucrat" (*Analects* XX:2).

This is not a good period to move unless it is to a distant location. If you do plan to move, however, avoid moving southeast or northwest. All other directions are permitted.

42 Take full advantage of your opportunities. You are in a fortunate period that favors moving up in rank, broadening your interests and business activities, taking on greater responsibilities, making investments, obtaining funds, traveling, meeting new people, attending business meetings, and improving your relations with those both above and below you. If you behave arrogantly, however, you will be courting eventual misfortune. Be humble. "Every day I examine myself on three points: whether I have been faithful in transacting business with others; whether I have been sincere in communicating with friends; whether I put into practice the lessons I have learned" (*Analects* I:4).

If you plan to move during this period, avoid moving southeast or northwest. All other directions are favorable.

43 Prevent corruption from developing. You are in a period when being headstrong, extravagant, ostentatious, overexpansive, or overconfident about anticipated profits and windfalls could spell serious disappointments. Nonetheless, this period favors financial growth through productive cooperation with others. Be willing to communicate intelligently to prevent misunderstandings from coming between you and your colleagues. Agreements and contracts could fall through at the last minute unless everything is carefully spelled out and agreed upon. "Virtue is not left to stand alone. He who practices it must have neighbors" (*Analects* V:25).

If you plan to move during this period, avoid moving east, southeast, west, or northwest. All other directions are favorable.

44 Exercise self-control. You are in a transitional period that may call for reorganization and reform. Some of your business activities may come to an end or take on a new direction, while other activities that have been lying dormant may show new life. Communication with others can be difficult and even critical. Try to ease up. By attempting to force your way, you will meet with serious resistance. You may be held back by circumstances beyond your control. Avoid disputes, and remain humble. "Cunning words and arrogant airs are not associated with true virtue" (*Analects* I:3).

If you plan to move during this period, avoid moving northeast, east, southwest, or west. All other directions are favorable.

45 Refrain from indulging in pretension. You could be taken by surprise. Favorable and unfavorable matters heretofore kept secret from you will come to light. Your secrets may become public knowledge as well. If your past business and financial dealings have been less than exemplary, you may be exposed and have to suffer the consequences. At worst you could risk a demotion, job loss, or a lawsuit. On the other hand, you could make surprisingly rapid progress, win the support of your colleagues and superiors, be promoted, or receive a surprise bonus, or if you are an artist, writer, or scientist, you may gain public recognition. Documents, signatures, meetings, and partings of the way are particularly significant in this period. Reflect on how ethical you are in pursuing your aims. "If riches and honor cannot be obtained in the right way, they will be lost. If poverty and meanness cannot be overcome in the right way, they will not go away. The superior man never acts contrary to virtue. In moments of haste, he cleaves to it. In times of danger, he cleaves to it" (*Analects* IV:5).

If you plan to move during this period, avoid moving north, northeast, south, or southwest. All other directions are favorable.

46 Keep within your limits and adapt to pressures in this uncertain and potentially stressful period. This may not be an easy time for your work, ventures, and business relationships, especially those that are just beginning. Stick to routines, and avoid entanglements. Avoid confiding in the wrong people. Misunderstandings and quarrels could lead to your eventual demotion or job loss. When you experience difficulties in communicating or negotiating with others, hold back and wait. "Faithfully encourage your friend, and guide him skillfully. If you find him resistant, stop. Do not disgrace yourself" (*Analects* XII:23).

If you plan to move during this period, avoid moving north, northeast, south, or southwest. All other directions are favorable.

47   Persevere. You are in a period characterized by gradual improvement. Use your money conservatively, and take time to work out your plans for the future and develop new business connections. Exercise caution if taking the lead in business ventures. Forcing your way against others will arouse enmity that will only cause you serious trouble in the future. Seize opportunities for future gain, however. "Studying without thought is labor lost; thought without studying is perilous" (*Analects* II:15).

   If you plan to move during this period, avoid moving north, northeast, south, or southwest. All other directions are favorable.

48   Refrain from cunning. You are in a period of rapid development that could bring you to great success or failure. Pay attention to details, and be courageous and open to surprises. This period favors being aboveboard, making decisions, taking initiative, and entering new territory. You can make surprising gains. On the other hand, underhandedness will jeopardize your status and could lead to your undoing. Be careful about how you interact with others. "When good government prevails in a state, one speaks and acts freely. When corrupt government prevails, one might act freely but never speaks freely" (*Analects* XIV:4).

   If you plan to move during this period, avoid moving north, east, south, or west. All other directions are favorable.

49   Follow your course with dedication while remaining self-restrained. In this period, positive activities begun in the past will come to fruition. This is an auspicious time for all business activities and travel. Good news is on the way. You will find others cooperative and friendly, and you will be helped by your superiors. Go forward confident of a promotion and increased prosperity. But avoid trying to force matters. To do so will seriously compromise your chances for success. Reflect on your need for moderation. "The man who is restless in his wants will proceed to rebellion, as will the vicious man, when you carry your hatred of him to the extreme" (*Analects* VIII:10).

   If you plan to move during this period, avoid moving northeast, southeast, southwest, or northwest. All other directions are favorable.

50 Be true to yourself. This period marks a turning point in which your affairs and activities from the past will come to a head for good or ill, while whatever you start now will take on great significance for your future. Although decisive action is correct and necessary, be discerning when communicating with others. Offending others will put you at a disadvantage and could spell your downfall. While you may be acclaimed by some for pointing out the faults of others, reflect on your own conduct. "If an official corrects his own conduct, what difficulty will he have in assisting in government? If he cannot correct himself, what has he to do with correcting others?" (*Analects* XIII:13).

This is not a good period to move unless it is to a distant location. If you do plan to move, however, avoid moving east or west. All other directions are permitted.

51 Be generous. You are in a fortunate period that favors moving up in rank, broadening your interests and business activities, meeting new people, making investments, obtaining funds, traveling, taking on more responsibilities, and improving your relations with your superiors. If you are willing to accomplish much without the expectation of immediate rewards, your position will be strengthened. Take inventory of your circumstances. "I will not be afflicted at men's not knowing me; I will be afflicted that I do not know men" (*Analects* I:16).

If you plan to move during this period, avoid moving southeast or northwest. All other directions are favorable.

52 Beware of temptations. You are in a period when vanity, ostentation, overspending, overexpansion, or presumption of huge profits and windfalls could spell big trouble. Nonetheless, this period favors financial growth through productive cooperation with others. Be careful to prevent misunderstandings from coming between you and your colleagues. Be alert to the possibility of deception. Partnership agreements and contracts could either fall through at the last minute or put you at an inevitable disadvantage unless everything is clearly spelled out and understood. You are essentially the cause of all that happens to you in this period. "When you see worthy men, think of equaling

them. When you see men of contrary character, turn inwards and examine yourself" (*Analects* IV:17).

If you plan to move during this period, avoid moving east or west. All other directions are favorable.

53 Be poised. You are in a transitional period that may call for radical changes. Some of your business activities may come to an end or take on a new direction, while other activities that have been dormant may display new possibilities. You may have to change your plans in the face of changing circumstances. Because communication will tend to be critical, avoid exerting undue pressure on others. Attempting to force matters will only arouse opposition. Try to work in harmony with others; to do so will lead to contentment. Always maintain presence of mind. "The superior man is at ease and composed. The mean man is always full of distress" (*Analects* VII:36).

If you plan to move during this period, avoid moving northeast, southeast, southwest, or northwest. All other directions are favorable.

54 Know who your friends are. You could be taken by surprise. Favorable or unfavorable matters heretofore kept secret from you will come to light. Your secrets could become public knowledge as well. If your past business and financial dealings have been questionable, you could be exposed and have to suffer the consequences. At worst you could be demoted, lose your job, or face a lawsuit. On the other hand, you could make surprisingly rapid progress, win the support of your colleagues and superiors, be promoted, or receive a surprise bonus, or if you are an artist, writer, or scientist, you may gain public recognition. Documents, signatures, meetings, and partings of the way count significantly in this period. You will receive the help and support of well-meaning colleagues and superiors when you need them. Watch the behavior of your colleagues. "Superior people are all-comprehending and not divisive. Mean people are divisive and narrow-minded" (*Analects* II:14).

If you plan to move during this period, avoid moving north, east, south, or west. All other directions are favorable.

55 Consolidate your position while working to create harmonious conditions around you. You are in a difficult period for work, ventures, business relationships, and partnerships, especially those that are just beginning. Stick to routines, and avoid confiding in the wrong people. Misunderstandings and quarrels could lead to your eventual demotion or job loss. If you remain calm and patient, however, others will come forward to help you when you need them. Watch others carefully. "The faults of men are characteristic of their upbringing. By observing a man's faults, it may be known whether he is virtuous or not" (*Analects* IV:7).

If you plan to move during this period, avoid moving north, east, south, or west. All other directions are favorable.

56 Be patient and sagacious. You are in a period characterized by slow, steady growth. Invest your money conservatively while taking time to work out your plans for the future and developing new business connections. Exercise wisdom when taking the lead in business activities. Forcing your way, just for the sake of having your way, will surely arouse enmity that will lead to serious trouble. On the other hand, if your motives are correct and your decisions appropriate, you will win the support of your superiors and will eventually be promoted. Cultivate discernment. "The love of goodwill without discernment leads to folly. The love of knowing without discernment leads to dissipation of mind. The love of sincerity without discernment leads to an injurious disregard of consequences. The love of straightforwardness without discernment leads to rudeness. The love of boldness without discernment leads to insubordination. The love of firmness without discernment leads to recklessness" (*Analects* XVII:8).

If you plan to move during this period, avoid moving northeast or southwest. All other directions are favorable.

57 Be flexible to avoid going to extremes. You are in a period of rapid development that could bring you to great success or failure, depending on how skillful you are. Pay attention to details, and be ready for surprises. This period favors making decisions, taking initiative, and entering new territory. Cre-

ative projects may blossom, and you could make some surprising gains. If you exercise good judgment while being as flexible as possible, you will find many opportunities for advancing your objectives. Be aware of the way you treat others, and the way others treat you. "An accomplished man is not a utensil" (*Analects* II:12).

If you plan to move during this period, avoid moving north, east, south, or west. All other directions are favorable.

58 Learn from your mistakes, and be courageous in the face of opposition. You are in a period when your positive activities begun in the past will pay off. This is an auspicious time for all business activities and travel. Go forward, in spite of difficulties, confident of an eventual promotion and greater prosperity. However, if you lose faith in the face of difficulties, or are unwilling to be flexible, you will be out of harmony with the time and may suffer a loss. Cultivate a positive outlook, and make yourself strong. "Not cultivating virtue; not thoroughly understanding what is learned; not being able to correct oneself; and not being able to change what is not good: these things distress me" (*Analects* VII:3).

If you plan to move during this period, avoid moving north, southeast, south, or northwest. All other directions are favorable.

59 Be gracious and modest. This period brings an auspicious turning point in your affairs in which your past efforts will come to a head, while whatever you start now will take on great meaning for your future. You may look forward to a promotion and higher salary. Nonetheless, be careful to treat others with respect. The misunderstandings and quarrels you bring about in this period could lead to your downfall. Open-mindedness will bring good opportunities. "There were four things from which the master was entirely free. He had no foregone conclusions, no arbitrary predetermination, no obstinacy, and no vanity" (*Analects* IX:4).

This is not a good period to move, unless it is to a distant location. If you do plan to move, however, avoid moving northeast or southwest. All other directions are permitted.

60   Be cooperative with those above and below you. You are in a fortunate period
      that favors moving up in rank, broadening your interests and business activi-
      ties, meeting new people, taking on greater responsibilities, making invest-
      ments, obtaining funds, traveling, and improving your performance and your
      relations with your superiors. How you relate to others will determine how
      successful you will be. "Fine words, a fawning appearance, and excess respect
      are shameful. To conceal resentment against a person while appearing
      friendly with him is also shameful" (*Analects* V:24).
          If you plan to move during this period, avoid moving east, southeast,
      west, or northwest. All other directions are favorable.

61   Rely on sound judgment. You are in a period when enthusiastic overexpan-
      sion, thoughtless overspending, or presumption of huge profits and windfalls
      could spell big trouble. Nonetheless, this period favors financial growth
      through productive cooperation with others, providing you exercise reason.
      Be careful to prevent misunderstandings from coming between you and your
      colleagues. Partnership agreements and contracts could fall through at the
      last minute unless everything is clearly spelled out and understood. If you do
      not rely on your better judgment, you could end up being blamed for failures
      and be demoted. Cultivate self-discipline. "He who requires much from him-
      self and little from others will keep himself from being the object of resent-
      ment" (*Analects* XV:14).
          If you plan to move during this period, avoid moving east, southeast,
      west, or northwest. All other directions are favorable.

62   Harmonize the divergent forces in your life and career. You are in a transi-
      tional period in which you may experience extreme ups and downs and be
      forced to reorganize your plans. Some of your business activities may come to
      an end or take on a new direction, while other activities that have been lying
      dormant may reemerge. Communication with others will not be easy. Try not
      to force your ideas on others; to do so will arouse opposition and enmity. If
      you remain calm and aboveboard, you can expect an eventual promotion and
      raise in salary. Be discreet yet unwavering in the pursuit of your goal. "If you

cannot be constant in your virtue, you will meet with disgrace" (*Analects* XIII:22).

If you plan to move during this period, avoid moving northeast or south-west. All other directions are favorable.

63 Do not treat others disrespectfully. You could be taken by surprise. Matters heretofore kept secret from you will come to light. Your secrets may become public knowledge as well. If your past activities were shady, you could be exposed and have to suffer the consequences. On the other hand, you could make surprisingly rapid progress, gain the favorable attention of your colleagues and superiors, be promoted, or receive a surprise bonus, or if you are an artist, writer, or scientist, you may gain public recognition. Documents, signatures, meetings, and partings of the way count significantly in this period. If you are unequal to the responsibilities you have taken on, you will run into trouble. Cultivate integrity. "Those who have no integrity cannot abide long in hardship or in ease. The humane rest in integrity; the wise desire integrity" (*Analects* IV:2).

If you plan to move during this period, avoid moving north, southeast, south, or northwest. All other directions are favorable.

64 Look to yourself for support. You are in a relatively inactive yet stressful period, which will not be easy for your work, enterprises, and business relationships, especially those that are just beginning. Stick to routines, and keep a low profile. Beware of confiding in the wrong people. Misunderstandings and quarrels could lead to your eventual demotion or job loss. Proceed slowly and cautiously to avoid unwanted trouble. "The student of virtue is not contentious" (*Analects* III:7).

If you plan to move during this period, avoid moving north, southeast, south, or northwest. All other directions are favorable.

65 Don't waste time in situations, and with people, that drain your energy. You are in a period characterized by slow, steady growth. Use your money conservatively, and take time to work out your plans for the future and develop

new business contacts. It is best not to take the lead in business ventures. If you do, be careful not to force your will on others; that will only lead to trouble. Allow others to express their ideas freely while being sagacious about what you say and write. Exercise discretion. "I am not concerned if men do not know me. I am concerned at my own want of ability" (*Analects* XIV:32).

If you plan to move during this period, avoid moving northeast, east, southwest, or west. All other directions are favorable.

66   Take advantage of expert help. Aim high. You are in a period of rapid development that could bring you to great success or failure, depending on how astute you are. Pay attention to details, and be ready for surprising developments. This period favors making decisions, taking initiative, and entering new territory. While your creative projects flourish, you will make surprising gains. This may be a most prosperous and successful time for you. Be discriminating when seeking help; use only the best. "Choose the upright and set aside the crooked, then the people will submit. Choose the crooked and set aside the upright, then the people will not submit" (*Analects* II:19).

If you plan to move during this period, avoid moving northeast, east, southwest, or west. All other directions are favorable.

67   Stay on course. You are in a period when positive activities begun in the past will come to fruition. This is an auspicious time for all business activities and travel. You will find others cooperative and friendly. Move forward, confident of promotion and greater financial gains. In general your activities will tend to increase during this period. Show gratitude to those who benefit you unless you are looking for trouble in the future. "Tze Lu asked how a ruler should be served. Confucius said, 'Do not impose on him and then turn against him.'" (*Analects* XIV:23).

If you plan to move during this period, avoid moving north, southeast, south, or northwest. All other directions are favorable.

68   Work assiduously. You are in a critical period in which activities begun in the past will come to a head for good or ill. Whatever you start now will take on

great meaning for your future as well. Be sagacious when dealing with others. Self-deception, misreading others, and resultant hostilities will put you at a serious disadvantage that could result in job loss. Persevere in the face of hardships. Cultivate self-reliance. "When a prince's personal conduct is correct, his government is effective without the issuing of orders. If his personal conduct is not correct, he may issue orders, but they will not be followed" (*Analects* XIII:6).

This is not a good period to move unless it is to a distant location. If you do plan to move, however, avoid moving north or south. All other directions are permitted.

69 Be resolute and upbeat. You are in a fortunate period that favors expanding your interests and business activities, taking on more responsibilities, making investments, obtaining funds, traveling, meeting new people, attending business meetings, and improving your performance and your relations with your superiors. Know what your goals are, and cooperate with those who can help you attain them. Avoid wasting time with those who will not help you. "Those whose courses are at variance cannot make plans with one another" (*Analects* XV:39).

If you plan to move during this period, avoid moving northeast, southeast, southwest, or northwest. All other directions are favorable.

70 Be realistic and willing to adapt. You are in a period when overexpansion, overspending, or presumption of windfalls and big profits could result in misfortune. Nonetheless, this period favors financial growth through productive cooperation with others. Be careful to prevent misunderstandings from coming between you and your colleagues. Partnership agreements and contracts could fall through at the last minute unless everything is clearly spelled out and agreed upon. Listen to what others have to say. If their ideas are helpful, use them. "When I walk along with others, they may serve me as my teachers. I will select their good recommendations and follow them, their bad ideas and avoid them" (*Analects* VII:21).

If you plan to move during this period, avoid moving east or west. All other directions are favorable.

71 Strive to know yourself and your place in the scheme of things. You are in a transitional period that may call for reorganization. Some of your business activities may come to an end or take on a new direction, while other activities that have been dormant may reemerge. If it becomes difficult for you to receive the information you want from others and to communicate effectively, refrain from forcing your way. Being unaware of yourself will set you up for serious difficulties. Know your limitations. "He who is not in a particular position has no right to meddle with the administration of its duties" (*Analects* VIII:14).

  If you are planning to move during this period, avoid moving northeast, southeast, southwest, or northwest. All other directions are favorable.

72 Strive to overcome whatever stands in the way of your creativity. You are in a period when you can make brilliant progress. You may be promoted or receive a surprise bonus, or if you are an artist, writer, or scientist, you may gain public recognition. Documents, signatures, meetings, and partings of the way count significantly in this period. If you are able to take corrective measures to overcome your obstacles, you will make significant strides that will lead to greater prosperity. Focus on essentials. "The aspirant whose mind is set on the way, and who is ashamed of poor clothes and poor food, is not fit to be talked to" (*Analects* IV:9).

  If you plan to move during this period, avoid moving north or south. All other directions are favorable.

EXERCISE

If you plan to make a permanent or long-term move, mark the indications of the year forecast, and fine-tune the time of your move according to the indications of the month forecasts. For example, if you want to make a lucky long-term move to the west, wait for a year that favors moving west, and in that year wait for a month that favors moving west.

If you move in a direction indicated as unfavorable according to your year forecast but favorable according to the month of your move, the fortunate effects of the move made that month will eventually wear off and leave you with the unfortunate conditions indicated by the forecast for the year. Conversely, if you move in a direction indicated as favorable according to your year forecast but unfavorable according to the forecast for the month of your move, the unfortunate effects of the move made that month will eventually wear off and leave you with the fortunate conditions indicated by the forecast for the year.

Of course, you can change your luck at any time by moving in a lucky direction, as indicated by year and month forecasts. I have observed this aspect of "directionology" of the nine star system closely. It does hold true. It is worth your attention.

ARRANGING YOUR WORK SPACE FOR PROSPERITY

HOW TO USE PART TWO

Successful strategy deals as much with space as it does with time. The way you arrange your work space will bear upon your degree of effectiveness and organization, and therefore upon the degree to which you can be successful. You might think of your work space as a sort of vehicle; it can take you anywhere you wish to go. The better situated and arranged it is, the farther it will take you.

THE SUPPLIES YOU WILL NEED

The supplies you will need to put the material in the coming chapters to use are a few photocopies of the floor plan of your work space and a compass (which you can find in most hardware or sporting goods stores).

YOUR FLOOR PLAN

Your floor plan doesn't have to be exact; however, it should be reasonably correct. If you are lucky enough to have a copy of the architect's original plan, use that. Otherwise you can most easily draw your floor plan on graph paper. If you don't want to take the dimensions of your work space with a tape measure, simply pace out the length and breadth of your space, estimating 3 feet to each step. Try to draw your floor plan on an 8½-by-11-inch sheet of paper for the sake of convenience.

If you are the owner or CEO of a business, you will find it most convenient to work with two floor plans: one of your entire place of business and one of your private office. If you are an employee occupying an office, work with the floor plan of your own office. If you occupy a cubicle, your floor plan should be of your cubicle. If you work at home, work with two floor plans: one of your entire home and one of your home office or the room in which you work. Even if you don't work at home, you can apply the material in the following chapters to your home. Its effect on your career will be highly advantageous.

THE COMPASS

To read a compass correctly, stand facing squarely toward the direction you want to read. Hold your compass level in front of you. Turn the whole compass case in your hand until the north end of the needle points to the letter *N* on the azimuth ring. (The azimuth ring is the ring of degrees—north, east, south, and west—printed on the plate of your compass.) The north end of the needle is either coated with green phosphorus or marked *N*. The earth's magnetic field causes this end of the needle to point toward the magnetic North Pole. To find your bearing just read the direction and degree straight ahead of you on the azimuth ring of the compass.

THE ELEMENT THAT RULES YOUR BUSINESS

Refer to your Personal Data List and note the element, or elements, corresponding to your business. If your business has more than one element correspondence, select the element you wish to work with. If one of the elements corresponding to your business is the same as the element of your birth star or one of your lucky stars, select it. For example, let's say that you were born under 6 Metal Star and that your business is in telecommunications. Telecommunications has correspondences to Wood, Fire, and Metal. Therefore you would select Metal to work with as the element corresponding to your business. For another example, let's say that

9 Fire Star is your lucky star and that your business is in stock and commodities trading. Stock and commodities trading has correspondences to Water, Fire, Earth, and Metal. Therefore you would do best to select Fire to work with as the element corresponding to your business.

Please note: If you are an employee working in a business in a specialized capacity, use the element that corresponds to the business in which you are working, not that of your area of specialization. For example, if you are a graphic designer working in a publishing house, the element of your business is Fire, for publishing, not Wood, for graphic designing.

As you read the coming chapters, you will need to make an all-important list of things to do to adjust your space. I shall refer to this as your Things to Do List.

CHI AND THE POSITIONING OF YOUR OFFICE

There are two ways to understand how chi moves through a space. The first is to imagine the chi as a stream, or current, that enters your space through the door, or doors, and windows, and circulates through the space, flowing out and back through the windows and doors. This idea, which should serve as a hint for your basic positioning of furniture, is illustrated in figure 4. Note how the chi follows the line of the walls and circulates around the center of the space.

(fig. 4)

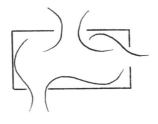

The second way to understand chi is simply that chi moves where you tell it to move. The chi is caused to move according to the arrangement of your furniture, decor, mirrors, colors, and lighting. It will be most active where the lighting and colors are brightest and will flow most smoothly along curved and straight lines. The more complex the arrangement of your furniture, the more complicated and potentially obstructed the movement of chi. The more obstructed the movement of chi, the more obstacles you will encounter in your work. The best

126

arrangement is the simplest and least cluttered. Clutter blocks movement, generates confusion, and results in stagnation.

THE GENERAL EFFECTS OF CLUTTER

In the context of the five elements, clutter is a negative expression of the element Earth; it indicates worry and neglect.

Clutter at the doorway is indicative of blocked access to the world. It means either that you are putting obstacles in the way of your goals or that you are burying yourself. Cluttered shelves overhead, or having things piled up to the ceiling, is indicative of obstructed yang energy, which ultimately results either in conflict with others or in feeling overwhelmed. Clutter at the money point of your space interferes with the development of your finances. Clutter at the power point of your space interferes with the growth and development of your career as a whole. Chronic clutter, or disorganization, on top of your desk is indicative of resistance to your work and of growing discontentment that can lead to trouble. Clutter under your desk crowds your legs and causes you to become irritable and/or confused. If you have things stored under your desk, even if they are neatly arranged in boxes, store them somewhere else. You will feel better. You can deal with clutter in closets by sorting out your things, discarding what is no longer useful, and organizing what is left in marked boxes, envelopes, or whatever containers are appropriate.

CLUTTER AND THE FIVE ELEMENTS

Clutter as viewed by the compass affects the corresponding elements in your work space as follows:

If clutter is found throughout your work space, in the middle area, or in the northeast or southwest area, it affects the element Earth and indicates too much worry. In addition, clutter in the northeast area causes plans and schedules to become confused, and clutter in the southwest area gives rise to all sorts of obstacles and overall bad luck.

If clutter is found in the west or northwest area, the element Metal is affected, indicating problems of communication and conflict with others over control issues. In addition, clutter in the west attracts the disloyalty of employees or co-workers, and clutter in the northwest attracts quarrels.

If clutter is found in the north area of your space, the element Water is affected, indicating a tendency to ignore problems that call for attention. In addition, clutter in the north brings accidents and business failures.

If clutter is found in the east or southeast area of your space, the element Wood is affected, indicating a tendency to become confused, indecisive, and irritable. In addition, clutter in the east gives rise to obstacles to growth and losses of money, while clutter in the southeast causes wasted effort and overexertion.

If clutter is found in the south area of your space, the element Fire is affected, indicating resistance to authority or abuse of power. In addition, clutter in the south attracts bad friends and quarrels.

No matter where it is, the obvious remedy for clutter is to remove it. The more open and well organized your space, the more easily you can breathe and get on with your work. Many times I have been called in by clients whose work spaces were cluttered and who were complaining about the sorry state of their professional and financial affairs. But once their work spaces were decluttered and reorganized, they saw their businesses and finances pick up dramatically. There's nothing magical to it. When your mind is clear, you know what you're doing.

POSITIONING YOUR OFFICE OR WORK AREA

If you work in a corporation, you probably have no say about the position of your office or cubicle. If you do have a say, choose the office or cubicle that has the best light and that is situated in the best possible current of chi; use your intuition. You should also choose the office or cubicle that allows you to sit with a compass direction in harmony with your birth star, or of one of your lucky stars, to your back. Other important considerations will be discussed in the upcoming chapters. If you are a CEO who can affect the overall design of the workplace, see Chapter 15. If you work at home, consider the following situations.

YOUR HOME OFFICE

Depending on its use, your home office should be either close to the front door or in a secluded area of your home. If you receive clients or customers, the best place for your office is close to the front door. Because a home-based business that receives clients and customers, or traffic, is yang by nature, it should be located in the most yang area of your home, namely, in a front room. Also, a home-based business that receives clients should be kept completely separate from the more private areas of your home. If your work requires quiet concentration—if you are a writer, artist, or researcher—your office should be in a secluded area of your home.

Since your office is in your home, you can apply all the guidelines in Part Two of this book to your entire home as well as to your home office.

YOUR STUDIO APARTMENT

If you live and work in a studio apartment, keep your work and sleeping areas completely separate. While remembering that you should place your bed in the quietest and most secluded area of your studio, position your work area where it will not upset your sleep. In order of importance, the placement of your bed comes first and the placement of your desk comes second.

Place neither your bed nor your desk in direct line with your door. If clients come to your studio apartment, you will need to protect your sleeping area from all the random and chaotic energy they bring in. You can do this with quartz crystals.

Obtain four fairly large quartz crystals. They should be about as big as the palm of your hand and should be natural, not polished. Bring your crystals to a sink. Let the cold water run until it is as cold as possible. Now visualize a blue-white light over your head. See the light coming down through the top of your head to the center of your chest, then radiating out so that the light completely surrounds you. Take your four crystals and run the cold water over them, saying silently or out loud, three times, "I will all confusion to run out of these crystals, that they be purified and ready to serve my purpose."

Once this is done, bring the crystals to your sleeping area. Put them on your bed. Stand quietly, and breathe calmly. Visualize the blue-white light emanating from your heart and entirely surrounding you. Take one of the crystals in your right hand if you are right-handed, or in your left hand if you are left-handed, and positively charge it. Breathe calmly and concentrate. With your mind, send the blue-white light through your hand into the crystal. Then visualize the light emanating like a flame from the crystal. See the crystal glow with the blue-white flame. Repeat this process with each of the remaining crystals.

When you have accomplished this, place the four crystals under your bed at its four corners and out of sight. If you sleep on a futon, place the crystals around the general area the futon takes up when unfolded.

Once you have properly placed your crystals on the floor, visualize a force field of blue-white light being formed around your sleeping area. Say to yourself, or out loud, "I will this force field to keep all negative energies away from my bed, and to let in only good, healing energies. And it is done." You can repeat this practice every month. If you follow the phases of the moon, the best time to do this is at full moon, when the psychic energy is strongest.

YOUR ONE-BEDROOM APARTMENT

If you live in a one-bedroom apartment, keep your work out of your bedroom. If you don't want your work to overwhelm you, keep all your file cabinets, papers, desk, computer, and other materials associated with your work in the living room. Keep your work and entertaining areas in the living room completely separate. The more logically you organize the work, living, and sleeping areas of your home, the more confident you will feel about yourself and your work.

EXERCISES

- Remove all clutter from your work space. Take out everything that doesn't belong in your work space, and organize all your papers and things that do belong there. The better organized you are, the more efficiently you will be able to work.

- Take a copy of your floor plan and experiment with sketching in the stream of chi, as was illustrated in figure 4. Can you come up with ideas about how to arrange your furniture to follow the natural flow of the chi in your space? Lightly pencil your ideas on your floor plan and in your Things to Do List. Wait until you have entirely read Part Two before you make your final decisions, however.

chapter 8

THE DOOR

In feng shui the doorway is one of the most important features to be considered in any space. Not only does the placement of the door determine whether the chi of the space is good or bad but it also determines which of the five elements (Water, Wood, Fire, Earth, Metal) rules the space. To put it most simply, the situation of the doorway contributes to the ease or difficulty, success or failure, of a business.

If you are the owner or CEO of a business, look at the main doorway to your workplace first and the doorway to your private office second. If you are an employee, look at the doorway to your office or the entrance to your cubicle. If you work at home, look at the main door to your home first and the doorway to your home office, study, living room, or other room where you work second. If you live in an apartment, the main door to your home is the door to your apartment, not the door to the building. If you live in a private house, the main door to your home is the front door of your house, not the garage door, side door, or back door, even if you use one of these doors most of the time.

THE MAIN DOOR IN RELATION TO THE OUTSIDE

Sha is a destructive form of chi that is generated by various configurations of objects, roads, buildings, and so on. Sha, sometimes called secret arrows, literally meaning "killing force," undermines luck and causes losses of money. In feng shui, sha is one of the most important things to look out for. If the main door to your workplace opens directly to the outside of the building, stand in the doorway looking out, and search for any of the following causes of sha.

- The doorway should not be blocked or obstructed. Obstructions hinder movement and generate obstacles to the flow of business. Remove all obstructions and clutter from around the doorway.
- The main door should not face a building that is situated at an angle, as shown in figure 5.
- The main door should not face a road that runs directly toward it or away from it, as shown in figure 6.
- The main door should not face a curved blade, or U-shaped road or over-pass with its curved edge slicing against the door, as shown in figure 7.
- The main door should not face part of another building and part of an empty lot, as shown in figure 8.
- The main door should not face any sharp object pointing directly at the door.
- The main door should not face a configuration of two buildings in which the one in back is slightly higher than the one in front, as shown in figure 9. This configuration symbolizes a thief.
- The main door should not face a single building that towers over all its neighbors. Such a building symbolizes enemies.
- The main door should not face a configuration of two buildings separated by a narrow alley, as shown in figure 10. This configuration symbolizes broken luck.
- You should not be able to see the water towers on top of neighboring buildings from your main door. Called tiger's heads in feng shui, these visible water towers symbolize losses of money.
- The main door should not face a sewage plant or garbage dump.

If your doorway faces any of these problematic situations, put plants, such as evergreen shrubs, at the sides of the doorway, as shown in figure 11, to absorb the sha, and/or cut out Talisman 1 from the back of this book, mount and frame it in white, and hang it inside, near the doorway, to ward off the secret arrows coming

133

(fig. 5)

(fig. 6)

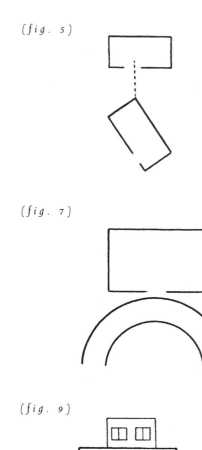

(fig. 7)

(fig. 8)

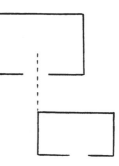

(fig. 9)

(fig. 10)

(fig. 11)

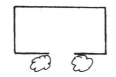

against your workplace. If you are an employee and have no say about the main door, you can hang Talisman 1 near the doorway inside your office or cubicle.

THE MAIN DOOR OPENING TO A CORRIDOR INSIDE THE BUILDING

If the main door to your workplace opens to a corridor inside the building, it should not directly face your neighbor's door, an incinerator, a stairwell, a bathroom, or a corner, as shown in figure 12. If your main doorway faces any of these causes of sha, cut out Talisman 1 from the back of this book. Mount and frame it in white, and hang it inside, near the doorway, to ward off the secret arrows coming against your workplace. If you are an employee and have no say about the main door, you can hang Talisman 1 near the doorway inside your office or cubicle.

(fig. 12)

THE MAIN DOOR IN RELATION TO THE INSIDE OF YOUR WORKPLACE

Now stand in your doorway looking into your workplace, and search for any of the following causes of sha.

- The doorway should not be directly in line with a staircase. Stairs running directly down to the main door symbolize money running out the door. If you have this problem, make sure the stairway is brightly lit at the upper landing to draw up the chi, and hang a mirror just to the side of the door to reflect the stairs and reverse the movement of the chi from downward to upward.
- The doorway should not face a corner, as shown in figure 12. If it does, put a mirror or decorative object on the extended wall, as shown in figure 13.

135

(*fig. 13*)

- The doorway should not directly face a freestanding structural column. If it does, attach full-length mirrors to all sides of the column and/or put an attractive standing plant in front of the column to camouflage it.
- The doorway should not be obstructed by a wall, making the entrance feel cramped and narrow. If the doorway is obstructed, hang small pictures relating to the nature of your business on the wall opposite the door.
- The main door should not be directly in line with, and within view of, the back door. If it is, screen off the back door so that you cannot see it from the main door.
- The doorway should not face a bathroom, kitchen, water pipe, or sink. If it faces a bathroom or kitchen, put a full-length mirror on the outside of the bathroom or kitchen door. If the kitchen is open, use screens to camouflage it. If the doorway faces a water pipe or sink, screen them so they are not visible from the doorway.

THE DOOR TO YOUR OFFICE

Stand in the doorway of your office, facing out, to see if you have any of the following causes of sha.

- Your door should not directly face a staircase. If it does, put a plant or something green by the door to absorb the swift-moving chi flowing down the stairway.
- Your door should not be hidden and hard to reach. If it is, use lighting and/or a sign to make its position more obvious.
- Your door should not directly face your neighbor's door across the hall. If it does, cut out Talisman 2, mount and frame it in white, and hang it inside your office near your door.
- Your door should not be at the far end of a long corridor, as shown in figure

14. If it is, cut out Talisman 1, mount and frame it in white, and hang it inside your office in full view of the door to ward off the secret arrows coming against your doorway from along the corridor.

(fig. 14)

DOOR

THE ENTRANCE TO YOUR CUBICLE

Stand in the entrance to your cubicle, facing out, to see if you have any of the following causes of sha.

- There should be no clutter around the entrance to your cubicle. Clutter generates confusion and slows down progress. If you find clutter, clear it up.
- The entrance to your cubicle should not face a stairway directly. If it does, put a plant or something green near the entrance to your cubicle to absorb the swift-moving chi flowing down the stairway.
- The entrance to your cubicle should not squarely face the entrance to your neighbor's cubicle across the way. If it does, cut out Talisman 2, mount and frame it in white, and hang it inside your cubicle near the entrance

YOUR DOOR'S COMPASS DIRECTION AND CORRESPONDING ELEMENT

Your doorway faces one of the eight compass directions, which corresponds to one of the five elements. The element to which your door is aligned is the element that rules your space. You need to take a compass reading of your doorway to determine the element that rules your space. To do this correctly, stand in your doorway facing squarely *out*. The direction you find on the compass indicates the door's element.

- If your door faces **north**, your space is ruled by the element Water.
- If your door faces **northeast**, your space is ruled by the element Earth.

137

- If your door faces **east,** your space is ruled by the element Wood.
- If your door faces **southeast,** your space is ruled by the element Wood.
- If your door faces **south,** your space is ruled by the element Fire.
- If your door faces **southwest,** your space is ruled by the element Earth.
- If your door faces **west,** your space is ruled by the element Metal.
- If your door faces **northwest,** your space is ruled by the element Metal.

If the direction you are facing appears between two compass directions, figure 15 will help you determine which to use.

Looking at figure 15, you can see that north extends from 337.30 to 22.30, northeast from 22.30 to 67.30, east from 67.30 to 112.30; southeast from 112.30 to 157.30, south from 157.30 to 202.30, southwest from 202.30 to 247.30, west from 247.30 to 292.30, and northwest from 292.30 to 337.30.

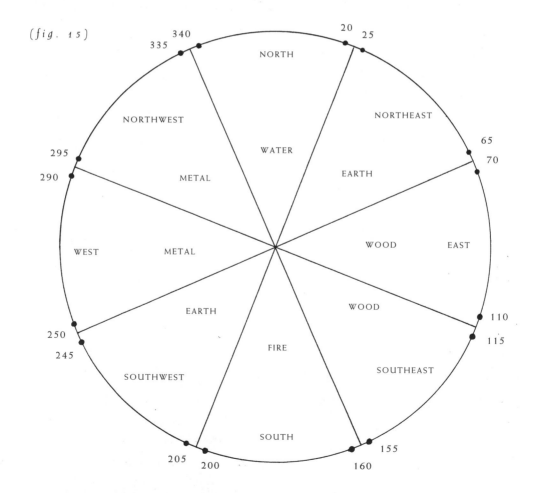

(fig. 15)

CREATING HARMONY BETWEEN YOUR BIRTH STAR AND YOUR DOOR WITH COLOR

Now that you have found the compass direction and corresponding element of your door, you can see if you are in harmony with your door's element and what to do to improve your luck if you are not. All you need to do is compare your birth star with your door's compass direction.

The following table shows the relations between the eight compass directions for a door and the nine birth stars. It also indicates the harmony or discord of the different combinations and what colors can be added to create harmony. If your situation calls for a harmonizing color, you can

- Hang a picture, poster, or sign featuring the desired color on a wall adjacent to the door
- Place a carpet in the entrance area

HARMONIZING WITH COLORS

DOOR FACES	BIRTH STAR	HARMONY/ DISCORD	COLORS TO ADD FOR HARMONY
North	1	Harmony	
	2	Discord	White
	3	Harmony	
	4	Harmony	
	5	Discord	White
	6	Harmony	
	7	Harmony	
	8	Discord	White
	9	Discord	Green or blue
Northeast	1	Discord	White
	2	Harmony	
	3	Discord	Purple or red
	4	Discord	Purple or red

Door Faces	Birth Star	Harmony/ Discord	Colors to Add for Harmony
Northeast (cont.)	5	Harmony	
	6	Harmony	
	7	Harmony	
	8	Harmony	
	9	Harmony	
East	1	Harmony	
	2	Discord	Purple or red
	3	Harmony	
	4	Harmony	
	5	Discord	Purple or red
	6	Discord	Black or navy
	7	Discord	Black or navy
	8	Discord	Purple or red
	9	Harmony	
Southeast	1	Harmony	
	2	Discord	Purple or red
	3	Harmony	
	4	Harmony	
	5	Discord	Purple or red
	6	Discord	Black or navy
	7	Discord	Black or navy
	8	Discord	Purple or red
	9	Harmony	
South	1	Discord	Green or blue
	2	Harmony	
	3	Harmony	
	4	Harmony	
	5	Harmony	
	6	Discord	Yellow
	7	Discord	Yellow
	8	Harmony	
	9	Harmony	

Door Faces	Birth Star	Harmony/ Discord	Colors to Add for Harmony
Southwest	1	Discord	White
	2	Harmony	
	3	Discord	Purple or red
	4	Discord	Purple or red
	5	Harmony	
	6	Harmony	
	7	Harmony	
	8	Harmony	
	9	Harmony	
West	1	Harmony	
	2	Harmony	
	3	Discord	Black or navy
	4	Discord	Black or navy
	5	Harmony	
	6	Harmony	
	7	Harmony	
	8	Harmony	
	9	Discord	Yellow
Northwest	1	Harmony	
	2	Harmony	
	3	Discord	Black or navy
	4	Discord	Black or navy
	5	Harmony	
	6	Harmony	
	7	Harmony	
	8	Harmony	
	9	Discord	Yellow

YOUR DOOR FORTUNE

Here is an interesting system of prognostication based on the combination of your birth star and your door's compass direction.

Looking at the table "Birth Star and Door Direction Combinations," you will find your door fortune number where your birth star number, from the top row, meets the direction of your door, from the first column on the left. For example, if your birth star number is 3, for 3 Wood Star, and your door looks to the south, you would read paragraph 21 in the fortunes.

Note: In this system 5, for 5 Earth Star, is not listed. Men born under 5 Earth Star should use 2 as their star number, and women born under 5 Earth Star should use 8. For example, a man born under 5 Earth Star whose door faces south should read paragraph 13, while a woman born under 5 Earth Star whose door faces south should read paragraph 53.

The prognostications in this system are meant only to call your attention to certain tendencies; they are not indicative of fate. Use them solely in a constructive spirit. Persevere where your door fortune indicates difficulties. Do not be complacent when your door fortune indicates ease.

BIRTH STAR AND DOOR DIRECTION COMBINATIONS

BIRTH STAR		1	2	3	4	6	7	8	9
DOOR	North	1	9	17	25	33	41	49	57
FACES	Northeast	2	10	18	26	34	42	50	58
	East	3	11	19	27	35	43	51	59
	Southeast	4	12	20	28	36	44	52	60
	South	5	13	21	29	37	45	53	61
	Southwest	6	14	22	30	38	46	54	62
	West	7	15	23	31	39	47	55	63
	Northwest	8	16	24	32	40	48	56	64

THE DOOR FORTUNES

1. Difficult position. Be meticulous at work, and take care to refrain from entanglements and quarrels. Do not take the goodwill of others for granted. Sincerity will lead to success.

2. Difficult position. Be flexible and patient. Stubbornness will cause you to lose the support and respect you need from others. When facing hardships and obstacles, seek expert help.

3. Easy position. Your efforts will be crowned with success here. Finding it easy to move forward and overcome any difficulties, you may look forward to promotions and favorable new beginnings.

4. Easy position. If you are considerate of others and know how to communicate effectively, your wishes will be fulfilled and your projects crowned with success. Troubles, if they arise, will soon pass away.

5. Uncertain position. While this position favors international trade and related affairs, it presages trouble if you are unequal to your responsibilities. Guard against developing financial difficulties.

6. Difficult position. Your inefficiency can create far-reaching problems. Being unequal to your responsibilities will lead to failure. Do not presume upon either your own authority or the kindness of your superiors.

7. Difficult position. Unless you make serious efforts to improve your skills, your progress will be impeded and you will lose precious opportunities. Be courageous when under pressure.

8. Uncertain position. If you are cooperative and considerate, your efforts will be successful. Be steadfast and orderly, and stay away from conflict.

9. Uncertain position. Associating with the wrong people and participating in quarrels will lead to misfortune. Avoid joining factions.

10. Easy position. Your efforts will win the appreciation and favor of your superiors, and you will gain a promotion, greater responsibilities, and prosperity.

11. Uncertain position. Taking the favor of your superiors for granted, feeling empty enthusiasm, and boasting about your connections will lead to unpleasant surprises. Don't press your luck.

12. Easy position. Your good efforts will lead to a promotion and greater prosperity. You could even serve as an adviser to your superiors.

13. Difficult position. Be careful not to let yourself be maneuvered into a stalemate. Your progress will be frustrated where your ambition is unjustifiable. Quarrels will lead to trouble.

14. Uncertain position. You will be fortunate if you follow, unfortunate if you take the lead. Leading from this position results in conflicts and losses.

15. Easy position. If your goals are clearly defined, you will win the support of your superiors and be promoted.

16. Difficult position. Meddling and trying to overreach your limits will result in trouble. Your progress could be obstructed, and you could reach an impasse. Avoid indulging in gossip, which will expose you to unpleasant insults and quarrels.

17. Uncertain position. If you are impatient, your progress will be difficult. However, if you can wait for good opportunities while patiently applying yourself to your work, you will be fortunate.

18. Easy position. If you are attentive, you will win the support of your superiors and be promoted.

19. Uncertain position. If you overreach your limits and go to extremes, you will run into trouble and suffer losses. If you calmly persevere while remaining flexible, you will have success.

20. Easy position. You may benefit through seemingly unfortunate or difficult circumstances. Be cooperative and sincere.

21. Easy position. You will make significant progress, gain recognition for your good efforts, and win the favor of your superiors.

22. Easy position. Your work will be crowned with success. You will gain financially, win the support of your superiors, and be promoted.

23. Easy position. If you set high goals for yourself, you will attain recognition, win the favor of your superiors, and be promoted.

24. Uncertain position. If your progress seems too slow for you, persevere and pay attention to details. If you give in to frustration and resentment, you will meet with trouble.

25. Easy position. If you cooperate with others, you will be promoted, make substantial progress, and enjoy financial gains.

26. Difficult position. The mistakes you can make by heedless and impulsive actions will cause you trouble. Pay attention to details.

27. Difficult position. Vacillating and confusion at work will cause you trouble. If you are hostile toward others, you may be demoted. Avoid disputes.

28. Uncertain position. If you are prone to worrying and procrastinating, you will lose opportunities and cause yourself a lot of trouble. If you are alert and decisive, however, you will meet with surprising luck.

29. Easy position. Your positive efforts will garner great success. Guard against the envy and jealousy of others.

30. Easy position. If you are kind and considerate toward those under you while being respectful of your superiors, you will win the support of both. You will be promoted and make favorable gains.

31. Easy position. Your work will bring you the recognition and support of your superiors. You will be promoted and make substantial financial gains.

32. Uncertain position. If you are attentive to details and avoid making glaring errors in your work, you will win the support of a strong ally. But if you are careless, you will run into trouble and could be demoted. Shun quarrels.

33. Uncertain position. Unless you make a point of being cooperative and considerate of others, you will run into difficulties. If you endeavor to win their support, you will be successful.

34. Difficult position. If you want to protect your interests, avoid quarreling with others. Exercise self-restraint.

35. Easy position. You can be confident of making strong progress and reaching your goals. Projects and ventures that get off to a good and happy start will be most fortunate in the end.

36. Easy position. If you have the opportunity to be innovative in your work, you will be most fortunate. Positive actions will lead to success.

37. Uncertain position. Unless you can put aside selfish motives and work for the benefit of all, you will be inviting trouble. If you can act impartially, you will ultimately make substantial gains and be promoted. Consider this position a stepping-stone.

38. Uncertain position. Persevere in the midst of fluctuating circumstances. Beware of trickery. If you are resourceful, you will be successful.

39. Uncertain position. Be willing to correct yourself to keep in balance. If you follow the golden mean and are positive in your actions, you will be successful.

40. Uncertain position. The immoderate use of power will result in misfortune. Exercise self-discipline and self-restraint if you want to be successful.

41. Uncertain position. You may become frustrated by the pressures you are likely to experience. However, if you want to keep out of trouble and succeed, be patient and stay within your limits.

42. Easy position. You will benefit through a partner. The key to your success here is cooperation. You will be promoted for your accomplishments.

43. Difficult position. If you become dissatisfied and make ill-timed moves, you will run into trouble. Be patient and cooperative.

44. Easy position. If you persevere, you will advance, be helped by your superiors, and be promoted. Your money will grow.

45. Easy position. Your difficulties will be followed by good fortune. Be cooperative; you will be helped by your superiors and promoted.

46. Easy position. Seize your opportunities. Go forward, confident that you will make sure progress and become increasingly prosperous.

47. Uncertain position. Be mindful of what and whom you are attracting. Dishonest and underhanded people can cause you a lot of trouble. If you offset your discontentment, and cultivate equanimity and harmonious relations with all, you will be favored by your peers and will be able to make sure progress.

48. Uncertain position. Be courteous to others and circumspect in your progress. Inflexibility and recklessness will lead to trouble.

49. Uncertain position. Seek the cooperation of others to achieve success. Being unaware and inconsiderate will lead to misfortune.

50. Easy position. Be self-possessed and cooperative to achieve success. You may be promoted to a high position.

51. Easy position. If you are adaptable and broad-minded, you will find many good opportunities for advancing.

52. Difficult position. Unless you exercise self-restraint and courtesy in the face

of opposition, you could be unduly discredited and suffer losses. Beware of envious colleagues.

53. Uncertain position. Be generous in spirit and broad-minded to be successful. Mean-spiritedness born out of fear leads to misfortune.

54. Easy position. A humane and courteous attitude will help you win the support of your superiors. You will be promoted and become increasingly prosperous.

55. Difficult position. Avoid entanglements. Think for yourself, stay away from gossip, and be as independent as possible to avoid being discredited and having to endure losses.

56. Easy position. Cooperate with those who are most enterprising. You will be promoted and make substantial financial gains.

57. Uncertain position. Use common sense. Your progress may be slower than you wish, and it may take a long time for you to become established. If, out of restlessness and discontentment, you quarrel with others or resort to under-handed means to get your way, you will meet with misfortune. If you are patient and methodical, however, you will make sure progress.

58. Difficult position. Be content and industrious to make consistent progress. Discontentment and restlessness will lead to hardship and loss.

59. Easy position. Strive to win the friendly cooperation of others and to surround yourself with able helpers. You will make strong progress, be promoted, and become increasingly prosperous if you do.

60. Easy position. Be industrious. If you pay attention to details, you will make sure progress, be promoted, and become increasingly prosperous.

61. Easy position. Be fearless and businesslike. Innovative and corrective measures to establish a better sense of organization will lead to success.

62. Uncertain position. Avoid inactivity. Positive efforts will lead to good fortune.

63. Easy position. Look upon all changes as ultimately fortunate. Your well-timed efforts will lead to promotion and increased prosperity.

64. Difficult position. Avoid harboring mistrust of others while appearing to be friendly. Trust yourself. Vacillating and cultivating wrong associations will cause you trouble. Cultivate equanimity and sound judgment.

EXERCISES

- If you find a cause of sha in your workplace, office, cubicle, or home office, make a note of it with its appropriate remedy both on your floor plan and in your Things to Do List. Wait until you have read through Part Two before you implement any of the remedies.

- Compare the reading of your door fortune with the astrological information you learned about yourself in Part One. Do any of the personality traits or tendencies indicated by your astrological readings show up in your door fortune? Frequently a person's environment reflects something significant about his or her personality. What personal lesson does your door fortune have for you?

WINDOWS

Because we function easily in surroundings that are pleasant, it stands to reason that irritating conditions, or causes of sha, in the environment can distract our attention and compromise the quality and progress of our work. Now let's look for secret arrows through windows and discuss the ways to neutralize their undesirable effects.

DETECTING SECRET ARROWS FROM YOUR WINDOWS

The following causes of sha, or secret arrows, when visible from your windows, can have subtle and negative effects on your nerves and contribute to your professional and financial problems.

- A road or driveway that runs directly toward or away from the window (as shown in figure 6)
- A sharp object, such as a spire, that is directly in line with or points directly at the window
- A building with a steep, pointed roof within view of the window
- A building falling into ruin within view of the window
- A dead or dying tree in front of the window
- Railroad tracks running across the view of the window

- Electrical or telephone wires running glaringly across the view of the window
- The window facing a curved blade, a U-shaped road or overpass with its curved edge slicing against the window (as shown in figure 7); by contrast, a curved road with its curving edge embracing the view from the window is good
- The window facing a tiger's head, or a water tank, on the roof of a neighboring building
- The window facing two neighboring buildings one behind the other, the building behind slightly higher than the building in front; the one giving the appearance of peering over the other at you symbolizes theft (as shown in figure 9)
- The window facing a solitary building that rises far above all the other buildings around it, symbolizing an enemy
- The window facing two high-rise buildings separated by a narrow alley (as shown in figure 10)
- A chimney or smokestack within view of the window
- The window facing elevated train tracks
- The window facing a hospital, funeral parlor, cemetery, church, temple, police station, or fire station
- The window facing anything that disturbs you

THE COMPASS METHOD FOR NEUTRALIZING SECRET ARROWS FROM YOUR WINDOWS

The way to neutralize, or remedy, any of the secret arrows you may have found when looking out your windows is quite simple; it involves using the compass and applying colors. As you will recall from Chapter 1, colors correspond to the elements: black and deep blue to Water; green and light blue to Wood; red, pink, rose, and purple to Fire; brown, beige, orange, and yellow to Earth; white, gray, and silver to Metal. We are about to select and use a color as the antidote to the element that contains the secret arrow you found outside your window. The element containing the secret arrow is determined by taking a compass reading of the direction you are facing when looking out the window. As you will recall, Water corresponds to north, Earth corresponds to northeast and southwest, Wood corresponds to east and southeast, Fire corresponds to south, and Metal corresponds to west and northwest.

Take your compass now and stand at the window through which you have detected the secret arrow. Look squarely out the window.

- If you are facing **north**, you are facing the element Water and will need to use something green or light blue in the window to neutralize the secret arrow with Wood colors.
- If you are facing **northeast**, you are facing the element Earth and will need to use something white, gray, or silver in the window to neutralize the secret arrow with Metal colors.
- If you are facing **east**, you are facing the element Wood and will need to use something red, pink, rose, or purple in the window to neutralize the secret arrow with Fire colors.
- If you are facing **southeast**, you are facing the element Wood and will need to use something red, pink, rose, or purple in the window to neutralize the secret arrow with Fire colors.
- If you are facing **south**, you are facing the element Fire and will need to use something brown, beige, orange, or yellow in the window to neutralize the secret arrow with Earth colors.
- If you are facing **southwest**, you are facing the element Earth and will need to use something white, gray, or silver to neutralize the secret arrow with Metal colors.
- If you are facing **west**, you are facing the element Metal and will need to use something black or deep blue in the window to neutralize the secret arrow with Water colors.
- If you are facing **northwest**, you are facing the element Metal and will need to use something black or deep blue in the window to neutralize the secret arrow with Water colors.

Once you have selected your color, you can apply it to your window in the form of curtains, shades, or venetian blinds. If you can't hang curtains or blinds of these colors, placing an object or objects of the desired color on the windowsill will work just as well. If you do not want to use colors, you can use the following substitutes: where green or light blue is indicated, use any type of plant except hanging plants and cacti. Where red, pink, rose, or purple is indicated, use an object that is triangular, pyramidlike, or pointed. Where brown, beige, orange, or yellow is indicated, use natural stones or objects that are square or cubic. Where white, gray, or silver is indicated, use metal sculptures or objects that are round or oval. Where black or deep blue is indicated, use objects made of glass or crystal, including natural quartz crystals.

If you are within view from a cubicle or work pool of a window over which you have no control and can detect a secret arrow through the window, you still can place a small object on your desk, or pin up a picture of the recommended color on the wall of your work space to neutralize the secret arrow. Although it is not absolutely necessary, try to put the object or picture in line between where you sit and the secret arrow.

The following vignettes will illustrate how this is done.

ELIZABETH

Elizabeth is a graphic artist who occupies an office in a large publishing company in midtown Manhattan. She can see a number of things, such as five tiger's heads, a steeply pointed roof, some spires, and two high-rise buildings separated by a narrow alley within view from her windows. When she takes a compass reading of her window's direction, she finds that the window looks to the northwest, which corresponds to the element Metal. Not wanting to put anything black or dark blue in the window of her office, Elizabeth chooses to place a large quartz crystal on her windowsill.

TODD

Todd is a trader who occupies a cubicle in a securities firm. From the entrance of his cubicle, he notices a secret arrow pointing directly at him from outside the window of the trading floor. Noting that the window faces southeast, the direction of the element Wood, Todd decides to put a predominantly red picture on the wall of his cubicle between where he sits and the secret arrow.

EXERCISE

Look out your window. What do you see? Do you find any secret arrows? If so, make a note of them in your Things to Do List. Next, take a compass reading of the window's direction by standing squarely in front of the window, looking out. If you have any question about the exact direction you are facing, refer to figure 15. Make a note of the window's compass direction in your Things to Do List. Once you have determined your window's compass direction, review the remedies discussed and decide how you will treat the secret arrow. Make a note of your solution in your Things to Do List.

For example, suppose you can see a tiger's head outside your window and find that the window faces north. In your Things to Do List you would write "secret arrow: north window." Then decide on a remedy and write it down. For example, "Hang light blue venetian blinds in window." Repeat this process for as many windows as you have. Wait until you have read through Part Two before beginning to implement your ideas.

chapter 10

THE SHAPE OF YOUR WORK SPACE

All things are expressions of chi, or spirit. Chi, in turn, expresses all things as forms. Nothing in our world exists without form. Forms are essentially concentrations of lines of force in space and time. Forms include everything from simple atoms to the most complex structures. It could also be said that forms give expression to chi. Following this reasoning, you can understand how the form, or shape of a place, expresses a quality of spirit.

Some shapes express more dynamic qualities than others, some are more conducive to productivity, some give more of a feeling of support than others, some are easier to understand and manage. In other words, different spaces will affect your fortunes in different ways for good or ill. You may find that one of the shapes described in this chapter resembles your workplace or office. If you are the owner or CEO of a business, apply the appropriate remedy to your entire workplace, and/or office, as needed. If you are an employee working in an office or cubicle, apply the remedy to that space. If you work at home, apply the remedy to your entire home or the room serving as your home office, as needed.

FAVORABLE AND UNFAVORABLE SHAPES

The best shapes for a living or working space, according to feng shui, are the square and rectangle. These are the most perfectly balanced and stable shapes and
are the easiest to work with.

Irregularly shaped spaces, such as L-shapes (figure 16), dustpan shapes (figure 17), complicated, irregular shapes with many corners (figure 18), trapezoidal shapes (figure 19), trapezium shapes (figure 20), triangular shapes, fan shapes (figure 21), and circular shapes can cause a variety of problems. L-shapes, dustpan shapes, and complicated, irregular shapes with many corners interfere with, and unbalance, the flow of chi through the space. Trapezoidal shapes, four-sided shapes that have two parallel and two nonparallel sides, and trapezium shapes, four-sided shapes without any parallel sides, create the feeling of lack of direction and confuse or weaken one's sense of purpose. The triangular shape generates anger and restlessness. Fan shapes with windows on the curved side, and circular shapes cause the chi to flow in and out of the windows too quickly, making occupants of the space distracted and careless. Let's look now at how these problems can be remedied.

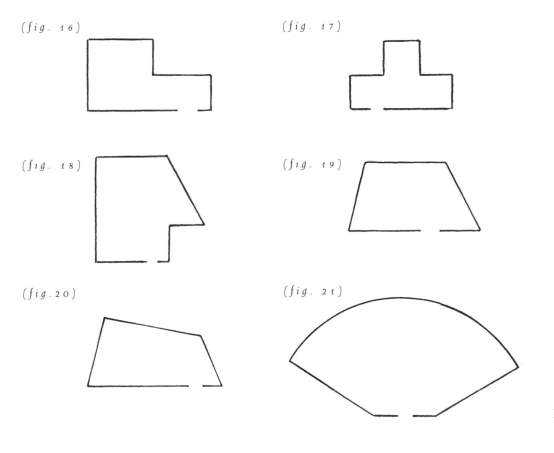

(fig. 16)

(fig. 17)

(fig. 18)

(fig. 19)

(fig. 20)

(fig. 21)

REMEDIES FOR UNFAVORABLE SHAPES

If the overall shape of your workplace, office, home, or home office resembles any of the shapes just listed, except the fan and circular shapes, take a copy of your floor plan and, starting from the outer points, complete a rectangle or square with a dotted line, as demonstrated in figure 22.

(fig. 22)

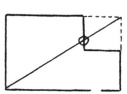

Next, draw diagonal lines from corner to corner and see where they intersect the existing walls, as shown in figures 23 through 27.

(fig. 23)

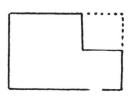

(fig. 24)

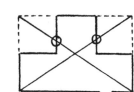

(fig. 25)

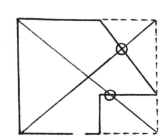

(fig. 26)

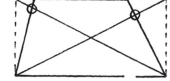

(fig. 27)

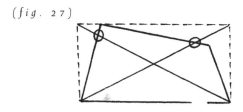

The points where the diagonal lines intersect the walls are most critical and are where you should place mirrors to remedy these unbalanced spaces. The other, more costly, way to remedy spaces such as these is to mirror entire walls, as suggested by figures 28 and 29.

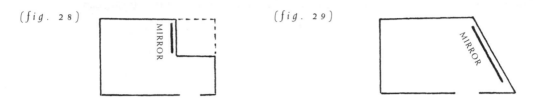

(fig. 28)   (fig. 29)

The mirror in figure 28 creates the illusion of the space expanding to fill in the missing area, as delineated by the dotted lines. The mirror in figure 29, placed on the slanted wall, creates the illusion of symmetry, balancing the chi of the entire space. The general rules for using mirrors as remedies for irregularly shaped spaces are as follows:

- Place mirrors on the walls backing the "missing areas."
- Place mirrors on slanted walls.
- Avoid placing mirrors too close to, and squarely facing, the doorway, as shown in figure 30, unless your intention is to keep people out.

(fig. 30)

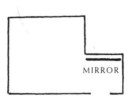

If your space is circular or fan-shaped, the only way you can effectively cure it is to hang curtains or blinds on all the windows. Sheer curtains or venetian blinds that let in plenty of light and allow you to see the view through the windows are perfectly fine.

SHAPES WITH PROTRUDED AND INDENTED AREAS

A protrusion is an area that appears to jut out of the main body of the space. An indentation is an area that appears to be missing from the main body of the space. Shapes with protruded or indented areas are quite easy to remedy once you know how to identify them.

Spaces with protruded and indented areas often resemble L-shapes or dustpan shapes. However, there are differences. Whereas you 'can tell an L-shape or dust-pan shape simply by looking at it, it is necessary to measure to determine whether areas are protruded or indented. For an area to be called protruded or indented, it must be no more than one-third of the length or width of the main body of the space, as shown in figures 31 and 32. In addition, for an area to be protruded it must exceed by at least one-third the length of the side of the space from which it extends, as shown in figure 32.

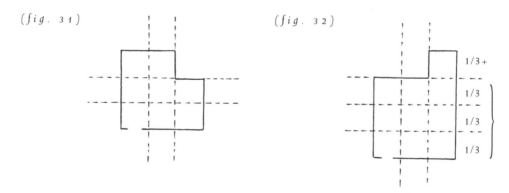

($fig.$ $3 1$)   ($fig.$ $3 2$)

Simple grids are superimposed on the spaces illustrated in figures 31 and 32. Figure 31 shows a space with an indented area, which takes up no more than one-third of the length or width of the main body of the space, as shown by the grid. Figure 32 shows a space with a protruded area, which takes up no more than one-third of the width of the main body of the space and juts out more than a full third of the length of the side from which it extends, as shown by the grid. If a space does not have true protrusions or indentations, it should be treated simply as an L-shape, dustpan shape, or other irregular shape as described in the preceding section.

158   Going one step further, we can judge protruded or indented areas according

to their compass directions. This simple method will reveal the secret meanings of the protrusions or indentations, along with the most appropriate and efficient means to remedy them. The first step in this method is to determine the central point of your space. The second step is to determine the compass directions from the central point of your space.

DETERMINING THE CENTRAL POINT OF YOUR SPACE

Take a copy of your floor plan. If the floor plan has an irregular shape, complete a rectangular or square shape with a dotted line, as illustrated in figure 22. Then draw diagonal lines from corner to corner, as shown in figure 33. The point at which the diagonal lines cross is the central point of the space.

(fig. 33)

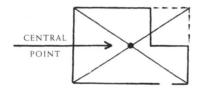

CENTRAL
POINT

DETERMINING THE COMPASS DIRECTIONS FROM THE CENTRAL POINT OF YOUR SPACE

The key to finding the correct compass directions for your space lies in determining the compass direction of your door. For example, if, while standing in your doorway with your compass, you look out to the east, the direction you would be facing if standing at the central point of your space looking toward the front wall would be east whether the door is directly in front of the central point or not. Figure 34 illustrates this.

(fig. 34)

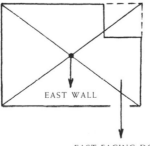

EAST WALL

EAST FACING DOOR

Once you have determined your door's compass direction, and, therefore, the direction you face when looking toward your front wall from your central point, you are ready to determine the rest of the eight compass directions. For the sake of judging protruded or indented areas according to their directions in space, draw eight spokes from the central point of the space of your floor plan. Figure 35 illustrates this step. If you are uncertain of the boundaries of the eight compass areas (north, northeast, east, and so on), refer to figure 15.

(fig. 35)

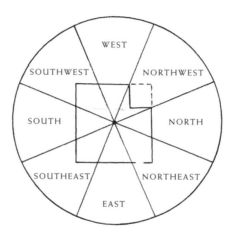

Once you have delineated the eight compass areas, write in what they are, as in figure 35. You can also see by this figure that the indented area of the space is to the northwest of the central point. This gives the key to the interpretation and remedy for this area.

Figure 36 shows the compass points of a space with a protruded area whose front door faces east.

(fig. 36)

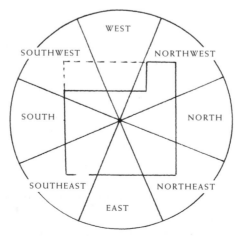

PROTRUDED AREAS

Let's look now at the meanings and remedies for the various protruded and indented areas. There are three remedies for each. You can apply any one, any two in combination, or all three together.

A space with the **north** area protruded attracts many friends as well as theft. Ventures led by the inexperienced working here are in danger of failure.

- Use green or light blue in the protruded area. For example, paint the walls green, put a green carpet on the floor, use green furnishings or green window dressings, or hang pictures with lots of green on the walls.
- Make sure the lighting in the protruded area is bright. Good lighting activates chi.
- Cut out Talisman 3 from the back of this book, mount it on a green mat, and frame it using green or light blue. Hang it on the north wall of the protruded area, or as close to the north as you can reasonably put it.

A space with the **northeast** area protruded favors research and development but could give rise to sharp financial ups and downs as the result of risk taking. Ventures led by the inexperienced working here can run into serious obstacles.

- Use white, silver, and/or gray in the protruded area.
- Make sure the lighting in the protruded area is bright. Good lighting activates chi.
- Cut out Talisman 4 from the back of this book, mount it on a white or gray mat, and frame it in yellow, gold, white, or silver. Hang it on the northeast wall of the protruded area, or as close to the northeast as you can reasonably put it.

A space with the **east** area protruded encourages impatience and recklessness. High-risk ventures here, especially if led by the inexperienced, can bring about serious financial losses.

- Use red and/or purple in the protruded area. For example, paint the walls with a tint of red or violet, put a red or maroon carpet on the floor, use bright or dark red furnishings (rosewood is fine), use red or violet window dressings, or hang pictures with lots of reds and/or purples on the walls.

- Make sure the lighting in the protruded area is bright. Good lighting activates chi.
- Cut out Talisman 5 from the back of this book, mount it on a red, rose, or purple mat, and frame it in green or red. Hang it on the east wall of the protruded area, or as close to the east as you can reasonably put it.

A space with the **southeast** area protruded can give rise to confusion, loss of focus, and overexertion. Ventures led by the inexperienced working here may result in financial loss.

- Use a lot of red and/or purple in the protruded area. For example, paint the walls with a tint of red or violet, put a red or maroon carpet on the floor, use bright or dark red furnishings (rosewood is fine), use red or violet window dressings, or hang pictures with lots of reds and/or purples on the walls.
- Make sure the lighting in the protruded area is bright. Good lighting activates chi.
- Cut out Talisman 5 from the back of this book, mount it on a red, rose, or purple mat, and frame it in green or red. Hang it on the southeast wall of the protruded area, or as close to the southeast as you can reasonably put it.

A space with the **south** area protruded may give rise to a good reputation and fame but will also give rise to fighting. Ventures led by the inexperienced working here will run into obstacles.

- Use earth tones in the protruded area. For example, paint the walls with a tint of yellow or beige, put a beige or brown carpet on the floor, use yellow, brown, beige, or orange furnishings (blond wood is fine), use beige or yellow window dressings, or hang pictures with lots of yellows on the walls.
- Make sure the lighting in the protruded area is bright. Good lighting activates chi.
- Cut out Talisman 6 from the back of this book, mount it on a yellow, orange, brown, or beige mat, and frame it in gold or brown. Hang it on the

south wall of the protruded area, or as close to the south as you can reasonably put it.

A space with the **southwest** area protruded favors women, not men. Ventures led by the inexperienced working here will be unproductive and will bring about losses of money.

- Use mainly white, silver, and/or gray in the protruded area.
- Make sure the lighting in the protruded area is bright. Good lighting activates chi.
- Cut out Talisman 4 from the back of this book, mount it on a white or gray mat, and frame it in white or silver. Hang it on the southwest wall of the protruded area, or as close to the southwest as you can reasonably put it.

A space with the **west** area protruded encourages friendly relations between co-workers but warns of declining fortunes. Ventures led by the inexperienced working here will tend to be unlucky.

- Use black or deep blues, and white in the protruded area. For example, put a black or deep blue carpet on the floor, use black or deep blue furnishings (walnut wood is fine), or hang black and white pictures or pictures of water scenes on the walls.
- Make sure the lighting in the protruded area is bright. Good lighting activates chi.
- Cut out Talisman 7 from the back of this book, mount it on a black or dark blue mat, and frame it in black or dark blue. Hang it on the west wall of the protruded area, or as close to the west as you can reasonably put it.

A space with the **northwest** area protruded favors men, not women. It also inspires leaders to become arrogant and gives rise to strife. Ventures led by the inexperienced working here will tend to be unlucky.

- Use black or deep blues, and white in the protruded area. For example, put a black or deep blue carpet on the floor, use black or deep blue furnishings (walnut wood is fine), or hang black and white pictures or pictures of water scenes on the walls.

- Make sure the lighting in the protruded area is bright. Good lighting activates chi.
- Cut out Talisman 7 from the back of this book, mount it on a black or dark blue mat, and frame it in black or dark blue. Hang it on the northwest wall of the protruded area or as close to the northwest as you can reasonably put it.

INDENTED AREAS

There are two remedies for each indented area. You can apply one remedy alone or both in combination.

A space with the **north** area indented invites accidents. Ventures led by the inexperienced working here are likely to fail.

- Use black or deep blue around the indented area. For example, hang black and white pictures or pictures of water scenes on the walls.
- Cut out Talisman 7 from the back of this book, mount it on a black or dark blue mat, and frame it in black or dark blue. Hang it either on the north or northwest wall of the indented area.

A space with the **northeast** area indented gives rise to poor planning and attracts strange and unexpected happenings. Ventures led by the inexperienced working here will meet with obstacles and sudden reversals.

- Use earth tones around the indented area. For example, paint the walls with a tint of yellow, beige, or orange, use these colors for window dressings, or hang pictures with lots of earth tones on the walls.
- Cut out Talisman 6 from the back of this book, mount it on a yellow, orange, brown, or beige mat, and frame it in gold or brown. Hang it on the northeast wall of the indented area or as close to the northeast as you can reasonably put it.

A space with the **east** area indented discourages growth and expansion. Ventures led by the inexperienced working here will result in financial loss.

- Use green and/or light blue around the indented area. For example, paint the walls green or light blue, use green or light blue window dressings, or hang pictures with lots of greens and light blues on the walls.

- Cut out Talisman 3 from the back of this book, mount it on a green or light blue mat, and frame it using green or light blue. Hang it on the east or southeast wall of the indented area.

A space with the **southeast** area indented is bad for business in general and gives rise to poor planning. Ventures led by the inexperienced working here will be fraught with confusion.

- Use green and/or light blue around the indented area. For example, paint the walls green or light blue, use green or light blue window dressings, or hang pictures with lots of greens and light blues on the walls.
- Cut out Talisman 3 from the back of this book, mount it on a green or light blue mat, and frame it using green or light blue. Hang it on the southeast or east wall of the indented area.

A space with the **south** area indented invites bad friends and gives rise to a bad reputation. Ventures led by the inexperienced working here will be fraught with obstacles and result in fights.

- Use red and/or purple around the indented area. For example, paint the walls with a tint of red or violet, use red, rose, violet, lavender, or purple window dressings, or hang pictures with lots of reds and/or purples on the walls.
- Cut out Talisman 5 from the back of this book, mount it on a red, rose, or purple mat, and frame it in red or purple. Hang it on the south or southeast wall of the indented area.

A space with the **southwest** area indented is generally unlucky but is especially unlucky for women and businesses that involve women's interests. Ventures led by the inexperienced working here will encounter serious obstacles.

- Use earth tones around the indented area. For example, paint the walls with a tint of yellow or beige, use window dressings that have earth tones, or hang pictures with lots of earth tones on the walls.

- Cut out Talisman 6 from the back of this book, mount it on a yellow, orange, brown, or beige mat, and frame it in gold or brown. Hang it on the southwest wall of the indented area or as close to the southwest as you can reasonably put it.

A space with the **west** area indented encourages disloyalty of personnel and bad relations between employees. Ventures led by the inexperienced working here will run into bad luck.

- Use white, silver, and/or gray around the indented area. For example, paint the walls white, use white, silver, or gray window dressings, or hang pictures that are predominantly white and gray on the walls.
- Cut out Talisman 4 from the back of this book, mount it on a white or gray mat, and frame it in white or silver. Hang it on the west or northwest wall of the indented area.

A space with the **northwest** area indented augurs weak leadership and invites quarrels. Ventures led by the inexperienced working here will run out of luck.

- Use white, silver, and/or gray around the indented area. For example, paint the walls white, use white, silver, or gray window dressings, or hang pictures that are predominantly white and gray on the walls.
- Cut out Talisman 4 from the back of this book, mount it on a white or gray mat, and frame it in white or silver. Hang it on the northwest or west wall of the indented area.

The following vignettes will illustrate how some of my clients have employed these methods.

BETTY

Betty, an illustrator, works in a studio whose shape appears in figure 37. Betty complained that her career seemed to be going nowhere, and she didn't know what to do. Seeing that one of her studio walls was slanted, I advised that she install a large mirror on it to create the effect of symmetry in the room. Soon after Betty followed my recommendation, an exciting and lucrative opportunity came her way, leading her into an area of creative work that she had long hoped for.

(fig. 37)

T
H
E

S
H
A
P
E

O
F

Y
O
U
R

W
O
R
K

S
P
A
C
E

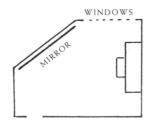

EDWARD

Edward is the head of a commodities brokerage firm. Looking for a way to increase his luck, he called me in to take a look at his place of business. Figure 38 shows the floor plan.

(fig. 38)

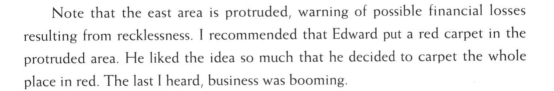

Note that the east area is protruded, warning of possible financial losses resulting from recklessness. I recommended that Edward put a red carpet in the protruded area. He liked the idea so much that he decided to carpet the whole place in red. The last I heard, business was booming.

KEITH

Keith, an interior designer, works in a space represented by figure 39.

(fig. 39)

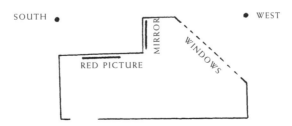

He called me in to look at his space because he felt discontented with the way his business was going. The slanted wall is a wall of windows, making it impossible to remedy it with a mirror. In light of this fact, I recommended that Keith treat the windows with white, silver, or gray. He chose to hang white venetian blinds and gray curtains. For the indented south area I recommended putting a mirror on one wall and a picture with reds and purples on the other. Soon after he made these simple adjustments and arranged the rest of his space to harmonize with them, Keith's attitude toward his business changed, and as a result, his business picked up considerably.

EXERCISE

Examine the shape of your work space and/or home. Is your space rectangular or square, or is its shape irregular? If it is irregular, go back over the material in this chapter to find out what the shape of your space signifies and how you can remedy it. Make a note of your findings in your Things to Do List. It may also help to make a note of your remedies on your floor plan. Before you make any final decisions on remedies, read the rest of Part Two.

TROUBLE SPOTS AND POWER POINTS

There is a direct correspondence between the condition of a space and the behavior and fortunes of its occupants. To put it plainly, the condition of your work space affects how well or poorly you are doing.

Here is a list of trouble spots and their remedies.

- A bathroom should not be located in the center of the space. The yin energy of the toilet will drain the space of its chi and cause financial losses. If you have this problem, put a full-length mirror on the outside of the bathroom door. Also place a plant inside the bathroom, or use the color green to activate the chi.

- The walls of your work space should not be warped; have protrusions, bulges, or bumps; or have holes or cracks. The dilapidated condition of your work space will depress your spirits and hinder your productivity. Repair all damaged walls and make sure they are as smooth and straight as possible.

- Your work space should not be too dark or oppressive. If you have too few or no windows in your space, make sure you install good lighting. If you work under fluorescent lights, change them to full-spectrum lights. Fluorescent lighting saps your energy. If your space is oppressive or stuffy, repair or install a new ventilation or air-conditioning system.

- Your work space should not have too many doors or windows. Too many doors and windows make it difficult to concentrate, and give rise to confusion, slow production, and hinder financial growth. Doors that are not essential should not be used. Where there are too many windows, cover them to create a feeling of containment. Venetian blinds or translucent shades are fine.

- There should not be exposed wires, air ducts, or water pipes running up the walls or across the ceiling of your work space. If you have these objects and cannot conceal them, cut out Talisman 1 from the back of this book, mount it on a white mat, and frame it in white or silver. Hang it on the appropriate wall of your space, as follows:

If you are the owner or CEO of a business, determine the placement of the talisman from the main door of the entire workplace. If you are an employee working in an office or cubicle, determine the placement of the talisman from the entrance to your office or cubicle. If you work at home, determine the placement of the talisman from the front door of your home, or from the door of the room serving as your work space. Remember, the way to determine the compass direction of your door is to stand in your doorway looking out.

If the entrance to your space faces **north**, hang the talisman on the west wall.

If the entrance to your space faces **northeast**, hang the talisman on the southeast wall.

If the entrance to your space faces **east**, hang the talisman on the west wall.

If the entrance to your space faces **southeast**, hang the talisman on the northwest wall.

If the entrance to your space faces **south**, hang the talisman on the west wall.

If the entrance to your space faces **southwest**, hang the talisman on the southeast wall.

If the entrance to your space faces **west**, hang the talisman on the north wall.

If the entrance to your space faces **northwest**, hang the talisman on the southeast wall.

- There should not be freestanding structural columns in your work space, as in figure 40. If you have such columns, and the space is large enough, use the columns to define work areas by putting up partitions or constructing walls from the columns, as in figure 41. If the space is too small, or if it is inconvenient to put up partitions or walls, place full-length mirrors on all sides of the columns and/or camouflage the columns with tall plants. Silk plants will do.

(fig. 40)   *(fig. 41)*

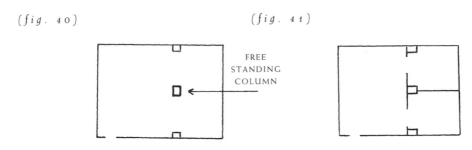

FREE
STANDING
COLUMN

- It is considered bad feng shui for a space to have long, narrow corridors. If it does, hang pictures or posters gallery fashion along the walls of the corridors, and make sure the lighting is satisfactory.
- It is considered bad feng shui for a space to have heavy beams running across the ceiling. If you have this problem and it is impractical to install a dropped ceiling to cover the beams, try to avoid placing your desk directly beneath a beam. If it is impossible to position your desk anywhere except beneath a beam, cut out Talisman 1 from the back of this book, mount it on a white mat, and frame it in white or silver. Hang it on the wall directly beneath the beam under which you are sitting.

THE MONEY POINT AND THE POWER POINT

The money point and the power point call for special attention. Bad conditions affecting these sensitive areas can undermine your business activities and finances. But when these two areas are in good order, your business activities and opportunities for financial growth will flourish.

FINDING THE MONEY POINT OF YOUR SPACE

Looking into any space from its doorway, the money point is at the far left-hand corner, as in figure 42.

(*fig. 42*)

MONEY POINT

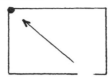

While your entire workplace or home has its money point, each office, cubicle, and room has its own money point as well. Therefore, look for your money point in the actual space in which you are working. If you are the owner or CEO of the business, locate the money point of your workplace from the perspective of the main door of the entire workplace, and the money point of your private office from the perspective of the door of your office. If you are an employee occupying an office or cubicle, locate your money point from the perspective of the doorway of your office or cubicle. If you work at home, you have two money points. Locate the money point of your home from the perspective of the front door of your home and the money point of your home office from the perspective of the doorway of the room in which you work. Both these points deserve equal attention.

FINDING THE POWER POINT OF YOUR SPACE

Looking into any space from its doorway, the power point is always diagonally opposite the doorway, as shown in figure 43. Sometimes the power point coincides with the money point, as shown in figure 44. When the door is exactly in the middle of a wall, the space has two power points, as shown in figure 45. In such a case the far left-hand corner, where the power point and the money point coincide, is the more important.

(*fig. 43*)   (*fig. 44*)   (*fig. 45*)

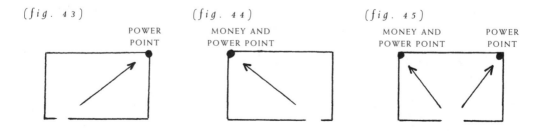

As with the money point, each office, cubicle, and room of your workplace and home has its own power point. Therefore, look for your power point in the actual space in which you are working. If you are the owner or CEO of the business, you have two power points. Locate the power point of your workplace from the perspective of the main door of the entire workplace, and the power point of your private office from the perspective of the door of your office. If you are an employee occupying an office or cubicle, locate your power point from the perspective of the doorway of your office or cubicle. If you work at home, you have two power points. Locate the first power point from the perspective of the front door of your home and the second power point from the perspective of the doorway of the room in which you work.

TROUBLE SPOTS AFFECTING YOUR MONEY AND POWER POINTS

Check your money and power points for the following trouble spots:

- A bathroom at the money or power point is unfavorable. The yin energy of the bathroom will drain your space of energy and the power to attract and accumulate money. If this problem exists, make sure the plumbing in the bathroom is in perfect condition, use the color green inside the bathroom, and put a full-length mirror on the outside of the bathroom door.
- Cluttering or obstructing the money or power point with papers, boxes, rubbish, or cumbersome objects is unfortunate. The money and power points must be kept as neat as possible so that the chi can circulate freely and easily in these important areas. Remove all obstructing or unwieldy objects and clutter from the money and power points of your work space.
- Windows closer than one foot to the corner at the money or power point, as shown in figure 46, will cause your money and power to fly out the windows. If you have such windows, hang blinds over them to contain the chi. Venetian blinds are fine.

(*fig. 46*)

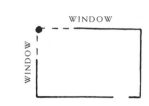

- A doorway at the money or power point, as shown in figure 47, is also unfavorable. The best remedy for this problem is to have the door moved, as shown in figure 48. Barring this costly solution, put a full-length mirror on the problem door facing into the room and/or place a tall standing plant beside the doorway. It will also help to keep the problem door closed as much as possible. A closet door at the money or power point of your space is no problem; just make sure the inside of the closet is neat.

(*fig. 47*)   (*fig. 48*)

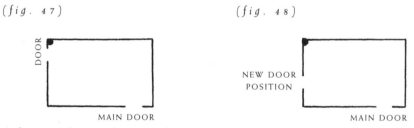

- A freestanding column at the money or power point, as shown in figure 49, obstructs the development of your money and power. If you have such a column, attach full-length mirrors to all sides of it and/or place a tall standing plant in front of the column to activate the chi.

(*fig. 49*)

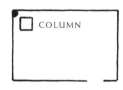

ENHANCING THE LUCK OF YOUR MONEY AND POWER POINTS

Once you have looked at your money and power points and corrected any problems, you can enhance your luck in the following ways:

- For the money point, cut out Talisman 8 from the back of this book. Mat and frame it with one of your lucky star colors, and hang it at the money point of your personal work space. If you work at a desk in an open area with no partitions, place the lucky money talisman on the upper-left-hand side of your desk. If your desktop is covered with glass, place the talisman, unframed, underneath the glass.

- For the power point, cut out Talisman 9 from the back of this book. Mat and frame it with one of your lucky star colors, and hang it at the power point of your personal work space. If your desktop is covered with glass, place the talisman, unframed, underneath the glass.

The following vignettes will show you how the fortunes of three of my clients improved after they took advantage of the remedies described in this chapter.

ROBERT

Robert, the director of a graphic arts business, was working in a space whose basic outline is illustrated in figure 50. Note that the bathrooms extend to the center of the space.

(fig. 50)

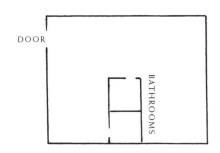

Robert was having a great deal of trouble controlling his finances. It seemed the more he worked, the more money he lost. I advised him to put full-length mirrors on the outside of both bathroom doors, to make sure the plumbing was in good repair, and to paint the insides of both bathrooms green. Not long after making these simple adjustments, Robert landed a job that gave him enough money to move his business to a better space.

BEVERLY

Beverly is on the administrative staff of a large hospital and works in an office with no windows. She complained that she was feeling nervous and stifled in her office and was having a great deal of trouble with her assistant. I advised her to change the lighting in her office from fluorescent to full spectrum and to add a couple of standing lamps. I also suggested that she put a green area rug (green is her lucky star color) on the floor, hang a mirror at the money point of her office, hang some pictures with lots of green on the walls, and bring in a comfortable chair for visitors. The overall effect of these suggestions was to give Beverly's office a feeling of ease and friendliness. She now felt pleased with her office and became more confident and relaxed. As a result of her improved attitude, Beverly found a new assistant, with whom she gets along very well. And, she says, people love to come into her office to talk with her.

SEAN

Sean is a stockbroker working in an office whose outline appears in figure 51. Note that the windows join at the money and power point.

(fig. 51)

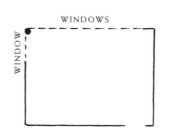

Sean complained that he was losing clients and that his business had been going downhill ever since he moved into this office. Realizing that it was not possible for him to move into another office any time soon, I advised him to cover the windows so that the money and power point would be closed in. I also suggested that he put a tall standing plant at the money and power point to raise the level of chi there. Sean decided to have curtains installed that were affixed to the corner so the corner would always be covered. He also added a large standing plant there. Soon after making these adjustments, he began to feel more encouraged about his business, and new clients started coming his way.

EXERCISE

In your Things to Do List, enter any trouble spots you found in your work space along with their remedies, as described in this chapter. Make a note of them on your floor plan as well. Also note how you might work with Talismans 8 and 9 from the back of this book. Wait until you have read the rest of Part Two before implementing your ideas.

ARRANGING YOUR FURNITURE AND PLANNING DECOR

Your furniture arrangement should allow the chi to flow as smoothly as possible. Always place your furniture and decorative objects in simple, balanced configurations. It is best to position your furniture parallel to the walls. If your room is very large, however, you can position some pieces of furniture diagonally in the corners to create a feeling of roundness.

Avoid creating obstacles by putting too much furniture in a room or by using furniture that is too large for the space. Also, avoid arranging your furniture in ways that interfere with, or complicate, normal routines. Use common sense.

It is always best to leave the center of your work space or room open and free from obstruction, as suggested in figure 4. Leaving the center of the room open allows the chi to circulate and helps relieve stress. If your work space or room is too small for the center to remain open, arrange the space so that there still is one open area. You can do this by leaving one wall or a significant part of a wall bare. If you have three walls filled with shelves, pictures, and other objects, and one wall empty, the empty wall will serve as a resting place for your eyes and will refresh your mental energy.

THE DESK

Depending on the function of your office, your furniture may include a desk, a table for your computer, a drawing board or table, bookcases, shelves, file cabinets, chairs and/or a couch, and works of art. The most important piece of furniture in your office is your desk, or your computer table or drawing board. The position of your desk is thus the first thing to consider. Try to avoid placing it in any of the following positions:

- Avoid placing the desk so that when sitting at it you directly face the doorway, as shown in figure 52. If you have no alternative, put large plants behind you.

- Avoid placing the desk so that the doorway is directly behind your back, as shown in figure 53. If you have no alternative, put up a mirror that allows you to see the doorway from where you sit. The mirror does not have to be large; think of it as a rearview mirror in a car.

- Avoid placing the desk so that the doorway is directly to your side, as shown in figure 54. If you have no alternative, cut out Talisman 1 from the back of this book, mount it on a white mat, and frame it with white or silver. Hang it on the wall opposite the doorway, as indicated by the arrow in figure 54.

- Avoid placing the desk so that you sit with your back to a window, as shown in figure 55. If you have no alternative, cover the window area behind you with blinds or plants.

- Avoid placing the desk flat against a window so that when sitting there you face directly out the window, unless the window looks to the north and no one can look in at you.

- Avoid placing the desk flat against a mirror so that when sitting there you directly face your reflection.

- Avoid placing the desk where you feel cramped.

- It is always good to sit with your back to a wall so that you look into the room. However, if you are working at a computer table or drawing board, or if the room is very small, you might prefer to sit with your table or desk against a wall. If you sit facing a wall, it is best to sit where you can see the doorway out of the corner of your eye, as shown in figure 56.

Figures 57, 58, and 59 show the best positions for your desk. In figures 57 and 58 the desk is placed at the power point of the room. (As you will recall, the power point is diagonally opposite the doorway.) In figure 59 the desk is placed in the most balanced position relative to the doorway and the entire room.

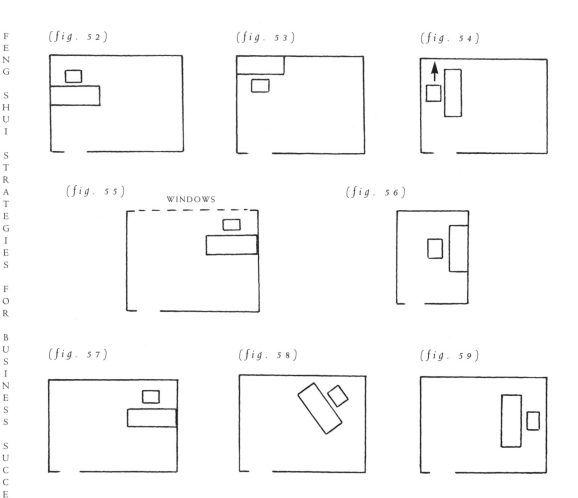

(fig. 52) *(fig. 53)* *(fig. 54)*

(fig. 55) WINDOWS *(fig. 56)*

(fig. 57) *(fig. 58)* *(fig. 59)*

If you share an office with one or two other people, follow the preceding guidelines for placement of their desks. Keep the following rules in mind. Avoid placing any desk with the doorway directly behind or directly in front of it. Try to avoid placing any desk with a window directly behind it. Avoid placing a desk directly against a window. It is fine to place a desk with the window to its side, however.

If two people are face-to-face in a room, one sitting with his back to the doorway or window and the other with her back to the wall, the one with her back to the wall will be in the more powerful position.

In an office where there are several desks, it is permissible to place one of the desks with the doorway to its side, as shown in figure 54. Do not, however, place the desks so that they squarely face each other from opposite sides of the room.

When people are forced to look directly at each other, the atmosphere always becomes discordant.

THE COMPASS ORIENTATION OF YOUR DESK

If your office space offers you more than one possibility for placement of your desk, try to place it so that the compass direction of one of your lucky stars, or a compass direction in harmony with your birth star, is to your back when you sit at the desk. For example, if you have 8 Earth Star as one of your lucky stars, position your desk so that you would sit with the northeast to your back. If your birth star is 7 Metal Star, position your desk so that you would sit with the west, southwest, northwest, north, or northeast to your back.

Considering the spatial limitations of a cubicle, your main concern should be to avoid having the entrance to the cubicle behind you when you are sitting at your desk.

ARRANGEMENT OF SECONDARY FURNITURE AND OBJECTS OF ART

In considering your file cabinets, shelves, bookcases, chairs and/or couch, and works of art, try to be as orderly and simple as possible. The furniture should be arranged so that your room feels balanced. It should be easy for you to move around, and all information should be easily accessible from your desk. Avoid cluttering the room and blocking the doorway and windows. It is best if bookcases and shelves are uniform in height. Do not hang your pictures and photos in a haphazard or zigzag way. It is best to keep the tops of your pictures in an even horizontal line. If you hang pictures one under the other, keep them centered; larger and smaller pictures should be arranged in well-balanced configurations. The more logically and simply you arrange your office, the more organized your work will be.

SYMBOLIC DECORATIONS

In addition to the symbolic images of your lucky stars and Talismans 8 and 9 in the back of this book, here are a number of traditional Chinese symbolic decorations you can use to enhance your professional and financial luck.

Symbol	Meaning
Bear	Strength and courage, protection against theft
Pot of coins	Prosperity
Conch shell	Prosperity
Deer	Wealth
Dog	Prosperity and protection
Dragon	Creativity and nobility
Bouquet of flowers	Wealth
Two goldfish	Success and abundance
Swallows	Prosperity and success
Toad	Wealth

You can decorate your office and home with statues, paintings, or photos of these symbols. The best places for them are the money and power points, and areas corresponding to your lucky stars. For example, if your lucky star is 1 Water Star, in addition to placing one of the symbols in the money and/or power point of your office, you could place it in the north area of your office.

MIRRORS AND LIGHTING

Mirrors are used in feng shui for a number of reasons. They can activate chi by brightening up a room; they can create the illusion of depth and give the feeling of symmetry in an otherwise unbalanced space, as illustrated by figures 28 and 29; and they can draw in pleasant views.

You can activate the chi of any room by putting mirrors to the sides of the windows or by hanging a mirror on the wall opposite the window, as illustrated in figure 60.

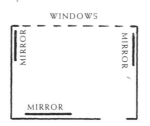

If there is a pleasant view outside your window, draw it in with a well-placed mirror so you can see the view from where you sit.

While the lighting in a workplace is best when it is bright, and it is good to use a desk lamp, the lighting should never be too harsh. It is a very good idea to change fluorescent lighting to full-spectrum lighting to avoid draining you of energy.

FISH TANKS

Fish, in Chinese symbolism, denote movement, prosperity, and success. For this reason aquariums have always been used to attract luck. If the idea of having an aquarium in your office or place of business appeals to you, use these guidelines.

The aquarium should be in harmony with either the element that corresponds to your business or the element of one of your lucky stars. Accordingly, if your business is in import-exports or any other area that corresponds to the element **Water,** or if your lucky star is 1 Water Star, place the aquarium against the north, east, or southeast wall on a white, black, green, or light blue stand. The shape of the aquarium should be hexagonal or rectangular. The combination of fish corresponding to the element Water is six of a dark color and one of a bright color.

If your business is in advertising or any other area that corresponds to the element **Wood,** or if your lucky star is 3 Wood Star or 4 Wood Star, place the aquarium against the north, east, or southeast wall on a black, green, or light blue stand. The shape of the aquarium should be rectangular. The combination of fish corresponding to the element Wood is eight of a dark color and three of a bright color.

If your business is in commodities brokerage or any other area that corresponds to the element **Fire,** or if your lucky star is 9 Fire Star, place the aquarium against the east or southeast wall on a green or light blue stand. The shape of the aquarium should be rectangular. The combination of fish corresponding to the element Fire is two of a dark color and seven of a bright color.

If your business is in foods or any other area that corresponds to the element **Earth,** or if your lucky star is 2 Earth Star, 5 Earth Star, or 8 Earth Star, place the aquarium against the southwest wall on a stand that is green and red, or light blue and red. The shape of the aquarium should be round or square. The combination of fish corresponding to the element Earth is ten of a dark color and five of a bright color.

If your business is in communications or any other area that corresponds to the element **Metal,** or if your lucky star is 6 Metal Star or 7 Metal Star, place the aquarium on the west, northwest, or north wall on a white or gray stand. The shape of the aquarium should be round or hexagonal. The combination of fish corresponding to the element Metal is four of a dark color and nine of a bright color.

If you cannot place the aquarium on an appropriate wall, it is better to do without it. Placing an aquarium somewhere else will only unbalance the chi of your place of business.

Because fish absorb negative chi, replace the fish immediately as they die. If you don't, the deterioration of the aquarium will attract bad luck. This will be all the worse if you place the aquarium at the money point of your office or workplace. As a general rule, you should not place an aquarium at the money point. If you do, be very careful to keep it in top condition.

Decorations used in an aquarium should be natural. Use only rocks and plants. Strange objects in an aquarium can spoil the attractive chi the aquarium generates.

In a corporate setting, the most logical area for an aquarium is the reception area or an executive's office. If you keep an aquarium at home, the best area for it is the living room, den, or home office. If you keep an aquarium in your office, however, do not put it where it will be in your way or distract you.

EXERCISES

- Take a copy of the floor plan of your work space. Make a sketch of the furniture placement in your office. Considering the guidelines in this chapter, position your desk, file cabinets, bookcases, visitors' chairs, and any other furniture you have for the space.
- Consider mirrors and lighting in your work space and how they can heighten the chi to give you more energy. Enter your ideas in your Things to Do List.

chapter 13

BRINGING HARMONY
WITH COLORS

Color is an extremely versatile way of remedying trouble spots. I have already described some of the ways colors are used to remedy trouble spots, which you will have noted in your Things to Do List. In this chapter I will show you how to use colors to harmonize your space completely with its ruling element as determined by the door's compass direction.

To apply this method, you will need to work with a fresh copy of your floor plan. If your space has an irregular shape, project its outlines to get a square or rectangle. Then pencil in two diagonal lines from corner to corner to determine its center, and mark in the compass direction of the doorway, as shown by figure 61. Next draw a radial diagram over your floor plan delineating the eight compass directions, as shown in figure 62.

(*fig. 61*)

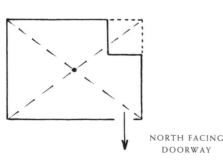

NORTH FACING
DOORWAY

(*fig. 62*)

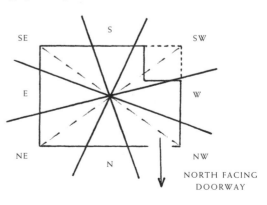

NORTH FACING
DOORWAY

If you are the owner or CEO of a business, first work with the floor plan of your entire workplace. After that work with a separate floor plan of your private office. If you are an employee occupying an office or cubicle, your floor plan should be that of your office or cubicle only. If you work at home, first work with the floor plan of your entire home. After that work with a separate floor plan of the room you are using as your home office.

Based on the compass direction of your doorway and the areas of your work space, you can balance the chi with colors as follows.

- If your doorway faces **north**, use white, gray, or silver in the northeast and southwest areas, and greens and/or light blues with a touch of black in the west and northwest areas, as illustrated in figure 63.

(*fig. 63*)

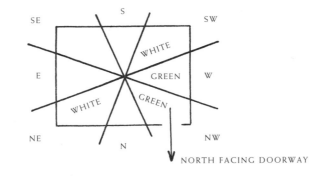

NORTH FACING DOORWAY

- If your doorway faces **northeast**, use reds and/or purples in the east and southeast areas, and white, gray, or silver in the north and south areas, with an additional touch of an earth tone in the south area, as illustrated in figure 64.

(*fig. 64*)

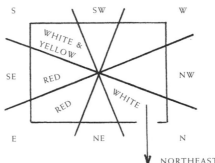

NORTHEAST FACING DOORWAY

- If your doorway faces **east**, use reds and/or purples in the southwest and northeast areas, and black or deep blue in the west and northwest areas, as illustrated in figure 65.

(fig. 65)

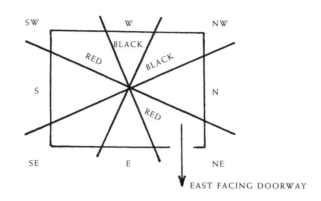

EAST FACING DOORWAY

- If your doorway faces **southeast**, use reds and/or purples in the southwest and northeast areas, and black or deep blue in the west and northwest areas, as illustrated in figure 66.

(fig. 66)

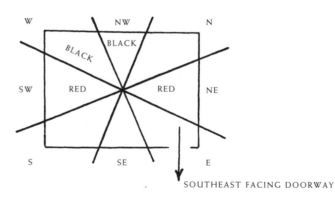

SOUTHEAST FACING DOORWAY

- If your doorway faces **south**, use white, gray, or silver in the southwest and northeast areas, and earth tones in the west and northwest areas, as illustrated in figure 67.

(*fig. 67*)

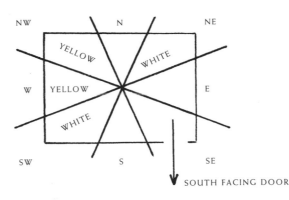

SOUTH FACING DOOR

- If your doorway faces **southwest**, use reds and/or purples in the east and southeast areas, and white, gray, or silver in the north and south areas, with a touch of an earth tone in the south area, as illustrated in figure 68.

(*fig. 68*)

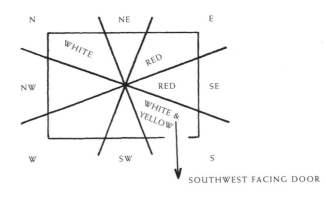

SOUTHWEST FACING DOOR

- If your doorway faces **west**, use greens and/or light blue, with a touch of black or deep blue, in the north area; black or deep blue in the east and southeast areas; and earth tones in the south area, as shown in figure 69.

(*fig. 69*)

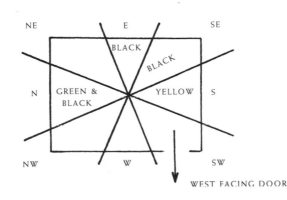

WEST FACING DOOR

189

• If your doorway faces **northwest,** use greens and/or light blue, with a touch of black or deep blue, in the north area; black or deep blue in the east and southeast areas; and earth tones in the south area, as illustrated in figure 70.

(fig. 70)

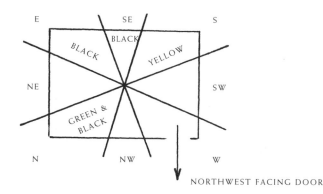

NORTHWEST FACING DOOR

There are a number of ways you can apply these colors to your space. You can paint the walls with tints of these colors, install carpets, use furniture that is painted or upholstered in these colors, or hang pictures or posters incorporating these colors.

The following vignettes illustrate how the color method described in this chapter can be combined with the color methods described in the preceding chapters.

GLENN

Glenn, born on October 10th, 1962, which gives him 2 Earth Star for his birth star, is an employee in a large corporation and occupies an office whose outline, with its compass coordinates, appears in figure 71. Glenn complained that he felt uneasy in his office and was having trouble concentrating on his work.

(fig. 71)

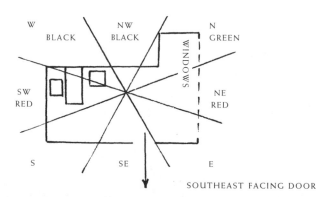

SOUTHEAST FACING DOOR

Note that the north area of Glenn's office protrudes, and that the compass direction of his doorway is southeast. You will recall that southeast corresponds to the element Wood. Referring back to the three cycles and figure 2, you will notice that the elements of Glenn's birth star and doorway, Earth and Wood respectively, are not in harmony.

There were three things to consider in adjusting Glenn's office. The first was the disharmony of his birth star with the element of his doorway. The second was the protruded north area, and the third was balancing the elements of the different areas of Glenn's office with the element of his doorway.

Referring to the cycle of mitigation (page 21), the conflict between the elements Wood and Earth is resolved by the element Fire. For this reason, I recommended that Glenn use the colors of Fire (reds, purples) by the doorway. He chose to hang a small picture with lots of reds and purples beside the door inside his office. Next, because the remedy for a protruded north area is to use greens or light blue, Glenn decided to put a large standing plant in the north corner, in addition to placing a number of smaller plants by the windows. Finally, since the southwest and northeast areas of his office needed reds and/or purples, and the west and northwest areas needed black to completely balance the space with the element of the doorway, Glenn hung a small red picture on the southwest wall, placed an amethyst geode on the windowsill in the northeast area, put a black desk and black chairs in the west area, and hung black and white photographs in the northwest area. To top it off, he hung Talisman 8 above his desk on the wall at the money point. The talisman was mounted on a mat of violet, a color corresponding to 9 Fire Star, Glenn's lucky star.

Once these simple adjustments were made, Glenn felt much happier in his office and was able to use his time more productively.

RONNIE

Ronnie, born on April 10th, 1970, is an employee in a large corporation and occupied a cubicle with the compass coordinates shown in figure 72. She called me in to look at her cubicle because she was angling for an important promotion.

(fig. 72)

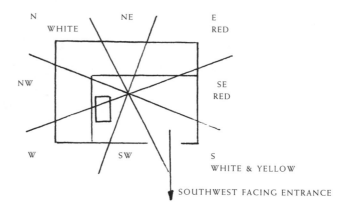

There were two things to take into account in adjusting the chi of Ronnie's work space. The first was the relation between the element of her birth star and the element of the entrance to her cubicle. The second was how to balance the different areas of the cubicle with the element of its entrance.

Ronnie's birth star, 3 Wood, was out of harmony with the Earth element of the southwest-facing entrance to her cubicle. For this reason, I recommended that she put something red or purple on the wall to the side of the entrance inside her cubicle. Ronnie chose to hang a picture of red flowers there. Next, since the east and southeast areas of her cubicle needed reds and/or purples, and the north and south areas needed white, gray, or silver, with a touch of yellow in the south area, Ronnie put pictures with reds and purples in the east and southeast areas, and a picture with predominant white and yellow in the south area of her cubicle. Since the north corner of the cubicle is both its money point and power point, she chose to hang Talisman 9 for success there, and because the north area needed white, she had the talisman mounted on a white mat and framed in silver.

After making these simple adjustments in her cubicle, Ronnie felt much more confident, was able to concentrate on her goal, and ultimately won the promotion she had been hoping for.

FRANK

Frank, born on September 12th, 1956, has a home-based network marketing business. The basic outline of his apartment with his home office is illustrated, with its compass coordinates, in figure 73, and the outline of his home office, with its compass coordinates, is illustrated in figure 74. Frank called me in to look at his home, hoping that his business might grow more quickly.

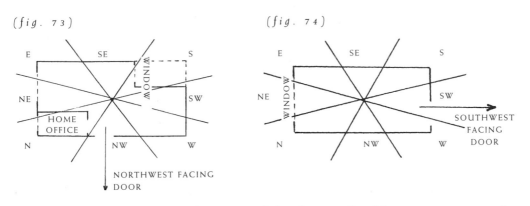

(fig. 73)   *(fig. 74)*

Note that the compass direction of the door to Frank's apartment is northwest, and the compass direction of the door to his home office is southwest, their corresponding elements being Metal and Earth respectively. Frank's birth star is 8 Earth. Because 8 Earth Star is in harmony with the Metal and Earth elements of the doorways to Frank's apartment and home office, there was no need to make any special adjustment among these elements. It was necessary, however, to treat the indented south area of the apartment and to balance the areas of the entire apartment with the Metal element of the northwest-facing front door, as well as to balance the areas inside Frank's office with the Earth element of its southwest-facing door.

Because there are windows around the indented south area of the apartment, I recommended that Frank use reds or purples for window dressings. He chose to hang purple curtains there, purple being the color of his lucky star, 9 Fire. Next, because the east and southeast areas of Frank's apartment needed some black or deep blue, and the north area needed some green, he put two Oriental carpets with deep blue backgrounds on the floor in the east and southeast areas of the apartment and placed a standing plant in the north corner of the office, the north corner of the apartment being the money point of the office. Finally, because the east and southeast areas of Frank's office needed some red and/or purple, the north area needed white, and the south area needed white with a touch of yellow, he had his entire office painted white, hung a purple picture on the southeast wall and a predominantly yellow picture in the south area, and hung Talisman 8, mounted on a purple mat for his lucky star, at the money point in the north area. It was no great surprise to learn that, soon after he made these simple adjustments, Frank's business began to pick up. He is now well on his way to the realization of his goal.

EXERCISE

If you have not yet done so, enter on your floor plan as well as in your Things to Do List the appropriate colors to balance the different areas of your work space with the element of its doorway. Think of ways to add the colors—by painting the walls, using carpets, window dressings, furniture, pictures and other objects of art, or plants, flowers, rocks, or crystals.

You are just about ready to begin using all the information you have gathered in your Things to Do List. Include whatever you have found in this chapter that applies to your office or cubicle in your Things to Do List. If you are an employee working in an office or cubicle, or if you work at home, read Chapter 14 before making your final decisions. If you are the owner or CEO of a business and are planning to redesign or reorganize your entire workplace, read Chapters 14 and 15 before making your final decisions.

USING YOUR
ENVIRONMENT

What I am going to describe to you here is a secret method whose principles stem from the ancient Chinese military use of feng shui and are often
implemented in architectural design by modern Chinese and Japanese commercial
firms. The controversial Bank of China building in Hong Kong is an outstanding
case in point.

The Bank of China building is a skyscraper whose upper parts are designed
with triangular shapes, creating sharp, bold edges. When the building was completed, the consensus in Hong Kong was that it was a disastrous piece of architecture that boded ill for the future of the bank. Contrary to public opinion, however,
the design is most ingenious. Viewed in relation to its surrounding buildings, the
Bank of China building rises like fire in a forest. Most of the surrounding buildings
are tall and rectangular, while the Bank of China building is distinguished by its
triangular shapes. The rectangular shapes correspond to the element Wood. The
triangular shapes correspond to the element Fire. Fire feeds on Wood. Wood supports Fire. This means that the Bank of China thrives on its environment in Hong
Kong. Better yet, because the element Fire corresponds to financial speculation, it
can be said that the Bank of China is destined to be a leader in investment banking
and rise to great heights of power, not only in China but in all the world. Thanks
to brilliant feng shui, the bank was given wings by the buildings surrounding it.

The principles used to support the Bank of China building can be applied to
any professional building or place of work. They can also be used by individuals

working in separate offices, cubicles, at desks in an open area, or in a home office. If you are the owner or CEO of a business, an executive or employee occupying an office, cubicle, or just a desk space, or if you work at home, you can use this method to advantage.

You will need to determine the following three things:

- The element that rules your business or the business in which you are employed
- The predominant or most outstanding element in the environment surrounding your place of work
- How to draw in the predominant element of the surrounding environment to support the element of your business

IDENTIFYING THE PREDOMINANT ELEMENT IN YOUR SURROUNDINGS

Take a good look out the windows of your place of work, or go outside and look at all the buildings that surround the building in which you work. By noting the colors and shapes of the buildings that surround your place of work you will be able to discern which of the five elements is most present in the environment. You will recall from Chapter 1 that each element has a corresponding shape and range of colors. Let's consider the buildings first by their colors.

Buildings ruled by Water are black or have outstanding features that are black. Buildings ruled by Wood are green or light blue or have outstanding features that are green or light blue. Buildings ruled by Fire are red, pink, or purple or have outstanding features that are red, pink, or purple. Buildings ruled by Earth are brown, sand color, orange, terra cotta, ocher, or yellow or have outstanding features of these colors. Buildings ruled by Metal are white, gray, or silvery or have outstanding white, gray, or silvery features.

With this information, make a list. How many buildings do you see? What are their colors? What are their corresponding elements? Do any buildings appear to be more outstanding than the others because of size or architectural details? What is the color of the most outstanding or impressive-looking building? What is its

corresponding element?

Now consider the buildings by their shapes and other significant architectural features. Buildings that have undulant architectural details or are made primarily of glass are ruled by Water. Buildings that are rectangular, skyscrapers with flat tops, are ruled by Wood. Buildings with pointed roofs, resembling inverted V's, and spires are ruled by Fire. Buildings that are wider than they are tall and have flat roofs, or a row of relatively low standing buildings of the same height with flat roofs, are ruled by Earth. Buildings with domes or cupolas, or many noticeable round or arched windows, are ruled by Metal.

With this information, make another list. How many buildings of each shape and outstanding architectural detail do you find? What are their corresponding elements? Is there a building or group of buildings that appears to dominate the view? What is its corresponding element?

Now tally up your lists of the colors and shapes with their corresponding elements. Which element is predominant? If you have any doubts, look out the windows or go outside again. Does any one of the buildings catch your attention right away? If so, what is the element of its shape or color? If you examine the shapes and colors of the buildings in the surrounding environment carefully enough, you will be able to discern which of the five elements is most present.

USING THE PREDOMINANT ELEMENT OF YOUR SURROUNDINGS

No matter what the element of the surrounding environment, there is always an element that will support your business. You will find that element in the following table. To use this table, first locate the predominant element of the surrounding environment in the left-hand column. Then locate the element that rules your business in the top row. You will find the element that supports your business where the appropriate elements in the left column and top row meet. For example, if the predominant element of your surrounding environment is Water and the element of your business is Water, the element that supports your business is Water. If the predominant element of your surrounding environment is Fire and the element of your business is Metal, the element that supports your business is Earth.

SUPPORTING ELEMENTS

BUSINESS ELEMENT	WATER	WOOD	FIRE	EARTH	METAL
ENVIRONMENTAL ELEMENT					
WATER	Water	Wood	Wood	Fire	Earth
WOOD	Metal	Wood	Fire	Fire	Earth
FIRE	Metal	Water	Fire	Earth	Earth
EARTH	Metal	Water	Wood	Earth	Metal
METAL	Water	Water	Wood	Fire	Metal

The supporting element can be brought to bear upon your place of work in many ways, ranging from simple decorative details to major construction. You can simply hang pictures, display interesting objects of art, or upholster your furniture using the colors of the supporting element. The following vignettes will illustrate these suggestions.

MATTHEW

Matthew works in a design firm, where he occupies a cubicle. He wants to strengthen his position with the company. Noticing that there are a large number of white and gray buildings within view of his place of work, Matthew correctly deduces that the predominant element of the surrounding environment is Metal. He also knows that the element corresponding to the design business is Wood. Using the table of supporting elements, Matthew finds that the supporting element for his business is Water and decides to hang a small picture of a water scene in his cubicle for luck.

LAURA

Laura is the head of a travel agency. She has just moved her business to a new location with the hope that it will thrive. Laura notices that there is a large, low-standing, flat-roofed building across the street that dominates the area and correctly judges the predominant element of the surrounding environment to be Earth. Knowing that Wood rules the travel business, she refers to the table of supporting elements and finds that the element Water will support her business in its present environment. Accordingly, Laura decides to have the chairs and other furniture upholstered in deep blue and puts pictures of water scenes on the walls for extra luck.

ROLF

Rolf owns a thriving international shipping firm and wishes to have a building constructed to house a new branch of his business. A site has been chosen in an environment dominated by a building that has a large, beautiful dome. Knowing that the dome corresponds to the element Metal, Rolf advises his architects that he wants his building to be faced with glass to reflect the dome so that the Metal element of the dome will support the Water element of his business.

EXERCISE

Now that you have singled out the element that rules your business, determined the predominant element in the environment surrounding your place of work, and located the element that supports your business in the table of supporting elements, enter what you have found in your Things to Do List. Include in your list a number of ways that you could introduce the supporting element into your workplace or work space.

chapter 15

DESIGNING AND RENOVATING FOR A CORPORATION

This chapter is addressed to architects, designers, and CEOs who are planning an office space for an entire company. If you are designing or
redesigning a workplace, aim for comfort of movement and simplicity of form.
Think of the space as a suit of clothes that either fits, letting people breathe and
move comfortably, or doesn't. Clean, straight lines always promote ease of
thought and smooth activity. Geometric patterns in either overall layout or decor
embody chi; they are like codes. Some patterns promote movement and positive
growth, while others promote stagnation and decay.

The geometric patterns in the design and decor of a workplace should be in
harmony with the element of the business. Here are the shapes that relate to the
elements ruling various businesses.

- If the business is ruled by the element **Water**, the most auspicious shapes to
  include in its design are undulant patterns, circles and ovals, and rectangles.
  The least favorable shape to emphasize is the square. The worst shape is the
  triangle.

- If the business is ruled by the element **Wood**, the most auspicious shapes to
  include in its design are undulant patterns, rectangles, and possibly triangles. The least favorable shape to emphasize is the square. The worst shapes
  are circles and ovals.

- If the business is ruled by the element **Fire**, the most auspicious shapes to
  include in its design are rectangles, squares, and possibly triangles. The

least favorable shapes to emphasize are circles and ovals. The worst shapes are undulant.

- If the business is ruled by the element **Earth**, the most auspicious shapes to include in its design are squares, circles and ovals, and possibly triangles. The least favorable shapes to emphasize are rectangular. The worst shapes are undulant.

- If the business is ruled by the element **Metal**, the most auspicious shapes to include in its design are squares, circles and ovals, and undulant patterns. The least favorable shapes to emphasize are rectangles. The worst shape is the triangle.

In all cases where the triangle is indicated as an auspicious possibility, bear in mind that it inspires aggression. The triangle should never be overused; it should be only an embellishment, never a structural element.

Figure 75 shows a detail of the floor plan of an unsuccessful design firm. Note the oval shape in the design. As you will recall, the design business comes under the element Wood. The reason this design did not work for this firm is that the chi of the oval shape, corresponding to Metal, has a destructive relationship to the Wood element of the design business. Had this been the floor plan for a business ruled by Water, it would have been perfect, since Metal supports Water.

(fig 75)

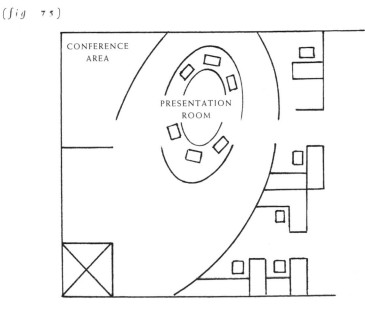

HALLS AND DOORWAYS

Hallways conduct movement. A hallway that is unusually long and narrow causes chi to rush through like an arrow. To remedy this, place either a series of pictures gallery style on both walls or a series of full-length mirrors at regular intervals along one of the walls.

A hallway that has doors directly facing each other, as shown in figure 76, especially if the hallway is narrow, will give rise to conflicts. Doors in a hallway are most favorably placed at regularly alternating intervals, as shown in figure 77. If your hallway has doors that directly face each other and you don't want to go to the expense of reconstruction, you can remedy the problem by hanging some brightly colored and interesting or amusing pictures along the walls of the hallway to divert attention.

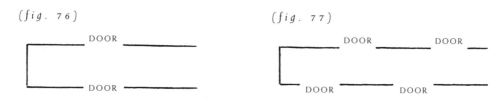

$(fig. 76)$ $(fig. 77)$

Doors that partially overlap, as shown by figure 78, also suggest conflict. The remedy for this condition is the same as that of figure 76.

$(fig. 78)$

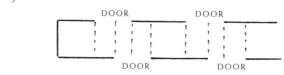

A hallway whose doors are crowded on one end, as shown in figure 79, also gives rise to conflicts. This problem can be remedied in two ways. The best way, provided the hallway is wide enough, is to place standing plants in the corners, as indicated by the arrows. Silk trees will do. The second way is to hang pictures of more or less subdued colors on the walls to the sides of the doors to calm the situation.

(fig. 79)

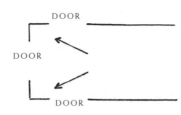

OVERALL ARRANGEMENT

The most important points to consider in arranging the workplace are the position of the main office, or CEO's office, and the ease of movement of personnel and operations. Once the location of the main office is determined, it will be relatively simple to figure out where everything else should go.

Short of considering compass directions, the ideal locations for the CEO's office are at the power and money points of the overall space. You will recall that the power point is diagonally opposite the main door of the space, and the money point is at the far left-hand corner of the space relative to the main door. If the power and money points coincide, so much the better.

The CEO's office should never be isolated from the main area of the workplace, or difficult to reach, as shown in figure 80. It should be at the greatest vantage point to all the operations of the business.

(fig. 80)

ENTRANCE

Because there is always more than one vantage point in a space, the office of the codirector or other top-ranking executive should be located at a vantage point that complements the location of the CEO's office. It is always good to position essential personnel within easy reach of the CEO's office. If it is not possible to have all of the essential personnel together, as in a constellation, the most essential personnel should be given the positions closest to the CEO, while those who are less essential should be farther away. What is most important is that everyone work together smoothly and with a minimum of wasted movement.

If the CEO's office is not at the money point of the space, the money point can be reserved for various other offices, such as the office of the codirector, the accounting office, the marketing office, the production manager's office, the conference room, or the presentation room.

Workstations and cubicles should be placed where they are more or less easily accessible to the executive offices. Cubicles located toward the center, or heart, of the space should not have high walls, because it is important to allow the chi to flow as freely as possible around and through the center of the entire space.

Special attention should be given to the reception area. The first impression your space makes on your prospective clients or customers will often determine whether they want to do business with you. The reception room always should be comfortable and decorated to inspire positive feelings about your business. Display such things as pictures that celebrate your line of business, pictures of your prize works, special awards, and so forth. (I know a successful commodities broker in Chicago who has a large poster in his reception room of a pig wearing four sneakers and a reversed baseball cap with the caption "Hogs are trendier than you think.")

USING THE COMPASS

If you have several choices for locating various offices, the compass method should help you narrow them down.

In any space areas of chi have either a positive or a negative relationship to the compass direction of the doorway. To find the positive and negative areas of chi in the workplace, take a copy of the floor plan and draw a radial diagram over it to include the eight compass areas (see figures 35, 36, and 62).

The positive areas are especially good for the executive offices, the accounting office, the marketing office, the production manager's office, the presentation room, the conference room, or any other office key to your business operation. The negative areas are good for things such as storage. If your space demands that you use areas designated as negative for your key offices and operations, make sure that you follow the color recommendations on pages 186 through 189 (see figures 63 through 70). These colors will transform the chi of the negative areas of your workplace, and make those areas more positive. Based on the direction you face when looking out the main door of your workplace, the positive and negative areas are as follows:

- If the main door of your workplace faces **north,** the positive areas are to the east, southeast, and south of the center. The negative areas are to the southwest, west, and northwest. The north and northeast areas are relatively neutral.

- If the main door of your workplace faces **northeast,** the positive areas are to the southwest, west, and northwest of the center. The negative areas are to the east, southeast, and south. The north and northeast areas are relatively neutral.

- If the main door of your workplace faces **east,** the positive areas are to the southeast, south, and north of the center. The negative areas are to the southwest, west, and northeast. The northwest and east areas are relatively neutral.

- If the main door of your workplace faces **southeast,** the positive areas are to the north, east, and south of the center. The negative areas are to the west, northwest, and northeast. The southwest and southeast areas are relatively neutral.

- If the main door of your workplace faces **south,** the positive areas are to the north, east, and southeast of the center. The negative areas are to the southwest, northwest, and northeast. The west and south areas are relatively neutral.

- If the main door of your workplace faces **southwest**, the positive areas are to the west, northwest, and northeast of the center. The negative areas are to the northeast and south. The southeast and southwest areas are relatively neutral.

- If the main door of your workplace faces **west**, the positive areas are to the northwest, northeast, and southwest of the center. The negative areas are to the north, east, and southeast. The south and west areas are relatively neutral.

- If the main door of your workplace faces **northwest**, the positive areas are to the northeast, southwest, and west of the center. The negative areas are to the north, southeast, and south. The east and northwest areas are relatively neutral.

THE OVERALL USE OF COLORS TO HEIGHTEN THE LUCK OF YOUR BUSINESS

Let's tie in all we have learned about the use of colors with the best overall color scheme for your workplace. The basic colors to use in decorating the workplace should either be in harmony with the element that rules the business or correspond to one of the lucky stars of the owner or CEO. Colors can be of any shade, as intense or as subtle as you wish. The recommended colors are as follows:

- If the business is ruled by the element **Water,** or if the lucky star of its owner or CEO is 1 Water Star, use any combination of white and black with grays. You can substitute deep blues for black.

- If the business is ruled by the element **Wood,** or if the lucky star of its owner or CEO is 3 Wood Star or 4 Wood Star, use any combination of greens with white and black. You can substitute deep blues for black and light blues for greens.

- If the business is ruled by the element **Fire,** or if the lucky star of its owner or CEO is 9 Fire Star, use any combination of reds and/or purples with greens or with earth tones. The range of reds to purples includes bright red, deep red, burgundy, maroon, rose, red-violet, blue-violet, magenta, and so on. You can substitute the lighter shades of blue for greens. Earth tones include all yellows, golds, ochers, oranges, tans, browns, sand colors, and beiges.

- If the business is ruled by the element **Earth**, or if the lucky star of its owner or CEO is 2 Earth Star, 5 Earth Star, or 8 Earth Star, use any combination of earth tones with reds and/or purples.

- If the business is ruled by **Metal**, or if the lucky star of its owner or CEO is 6 Metal Star or 7 Metal Star, use any combination of white and gray with earth tones.

The following vignette will show you how you can put some of the ideas in this chapter to use. It involves a small design firm whose director, dissatisfied with the way his business had been going and wanting to make over his workplace, called me in to help create a new layout. I had to come up with the best locations for the director's office, the administrative assistant's office, the general manager's office, the accounting office, the marketing office, the conference room, the presentation room, a network room, a reproduction and messenger room, the reception area, and twelve to fourteen workstations or cubicles. The basic outline and compass points of the entire space are shown in figure 81.

(*fig. 81*)

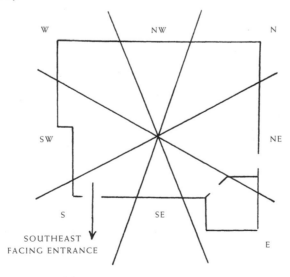

Noting that the power point of the space and area of positive chi are to the north, the north area was chosen for the director's office. It seemed most logical then, since the space allowed, to position the administrative assistant's office, the general manager's office, the accounting office, and the marketing office to the sides of the director's office. Once this was settled, I suggested putting the presentation room at the money point of the space, considering its proximity to the main entrance and obvious place for the reception area and the fact that the firm makes its money through presenting design ideas to clients. After placing the reception area, it was no puzzle to figure out where the conference room, the reproduction and messenger room, and the network room should go. The network room, a sort of conference area for employees, seemed best in the east area of the space, while all the workstations were put in the middle. The completed layout is shown in figure 82.

(fig. 82)

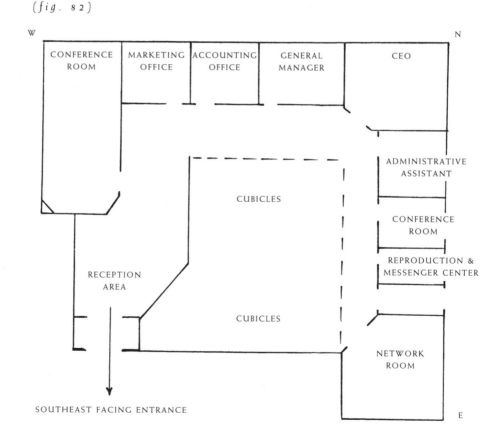

Since this is a design firm, Wood is its ruling element. So the colors chosen for the overall space were green for Wood and white and black for Water. Since the director's lucky stars are 6 and 7 Metal, he chose to have his office decorated in white, gray, and black, because Metal (white and gray) supports Water (black), and Water supports Wood.

The presentation room, placed in the west, was now in an area of negative chi relative to the compass direction of the main door. Because the element of the southeast-facing main door is Wood and the element of the west area is Metal, the color of Water, or black, was needed for the presentation room. This was easily provided by using a black conference table. The shape of the table, in keeping with the Wood element of the business, is rectangular.

It pleases me to know that this design firm is doing very well now. After they carried through these simple plans, the firm's business picked up, and it continues to grow steadily.

EXERCISE

- If you are designing, redesigning, or redecorating your workplace, what are the most auspicious shapes for your business to consider for your layout, furniture, and decorative motifs? Enter your findings in your Things to Do List.
- Are there any problems with the alignment of the doors in your hallways? What remedies can you apply to them? Enter your findings in your Things to Do List.
- Considering the power and money points of your space, as well as its positive areas of chi as determined by the compass, can you locate the best place for the CEO's office? Enter your findings on your floor plan as well as in your Things to Do List.
- Where will you position other key offices in relation to the CEO's office? Enter your findings on your floor plan as well as in your Things to Do List.
- How will you decorate the reception area to best advantage? Enter your findings in your Things to Do List.
- What colors will you use for your overall color scheme? Enter your findings in your Things to Do List.

chapter 16

PURIFYING YOUR SPACE

One of the great secrets to the power of feng shui lies not in the arrangement of the space but in the essential tuning of its chi. Chi from the heavens and the earth pervades any given space the same way chi pervades your body. Chi has yin and yang phases. Chi from below ground is predominantly yin. Chi from heaven is predominantly yang. In your body the left side is yin, and the right side is yang if you are right-handed. If you are left-handed, the left side of your body is yang, and the right side of your body is yin.

When the forces of yin and yang are brought into balance and harmony, everything in nature and in human relationships flourishes. When the forces of yin and yang become unbalanced and disharmonious, everything in nature and in human relationships disintegrates. When you are in excellent health and your chi is radiant, the yin and yang forces in your life are in balance. When the yin and yang forces in your life become unbalanced, your health and fortunes suffer.

If you wish to create a positive field of chi in your space, the first thing you need to do is make sure that you are in reasonably good health. Providing that you are, find a time when you will not be distracted; early morning is an excellent time.

Sit comfortably on a chair with your hips at the very edge of the seat. Sit up straight; do not allow your back to curve. Keep your neck straight. Imagine that your head is being pulled upward. Look neither up nor down but directly forward. Relax your shoulders, and rest your hands, palms down on your thighs, as close to your knees as is comfortable. Your body should lean neither forward nor to either side. Relax your body and lightly close your eyes, letting them remain just slightly open. Don't strain. Breathe naturally. If you smile gently, you will expand your third eye. Feel your smile deep down in your heart. When you smile from your heart, breathing normally with your body relaxed and at attention, you will naturally open to the cosmic chi.

Feel yourself breathing in life-giving chi from above, below, and around you all at the same time. Feel yourself breathing in the chi not only through your nose but through all the pores of your body. Feel the chi suffusing your body, and as you do, visualize the chi in your body becoming a pure white light. Exhale this light through all the pores of your body, as though you were radiating this light into and through your entire space—through the walls, the floor, the ceiling, the door, and the windows. When you feel complete, silently affirm that your space is totally filled with this radiant chi and will remain so for a specified length of time (one month is good). To finish this process, simply release yourself by dedicating its benefits to the joy and contentment of all sentient beings in the universe.

Do this practice both before and after you make changes and adjustments in your work space. If you do this before adjusting your work space, it will help you in making intuitive choices or decisions; your relationship with the space will have become positive. No matter where you work, try this practice at home.

I wish you success in using this book. It is my hope that it will contribute to your professional growth and prosperity. If you need my help by way of consultation, or if you are interested in having any of the symbolic images in this book painted for you by Zeng Xianwen, contact me at the following address: T. Raphael Simons, 545 Eighth Avenue, Suite 401, New York, NY 10018.

USING THE *I CHING*
FOR DECISION MAKING

The *I Ching*, or *Book of Changes*, is the oldest and most important book in Chinese literature. Originally composed by the emperor Fu Hsi in the twenty-ninth century B.C., the *I Ching* has served through the centuries both as a central model for Chinese philosophy, science, and political strategy and as an oracle. Consisting of sixty-four paired combinations of eight primary trigrams, whose names are Heaven, Thunder, Water, Mountain, Earth, Wind, Fire, and Lake, each hexagram of the *I Ching* represents a certain condition or aspect of nature as reflected in everyday experience. Many of the hexagrams have poetic titles, such as Difficulty in the Beginning, Biting Through, Possession in Great Measure, Preponderance of the Great, Fellowship with Men, and so on.

The *I Ching* is available in most bookstores. You may wish to purchase one of the many editions and consult it for your business decisions. In any case, I am presenting a method traditionally used by Chinese astrologers that does not require consulting the book itself. It is to be used for obtaining yes or no answers only. If carried out correctly and in an appropriately meditative spirit, it will help you make decisions on strategic moves. Although it may appear complicated at first, you will find it easy once you become familiar with it.

This method requires the use of five tables, found at the end of this appendix. To avoid confusion, always proceed step by step.

NOTE THE ELEMENT OF THE SEASON

On a piece of paper, write down the element corresponding to the season during which you are asking your question. You will remember that spring, whose element is Wood, falls, according to the Chinese calendar, between February 4th and May 5th; summer, whose element is Fire, falls between May 5th and August 7th; late summer, whose element is Earth, falls between July 23rd and August 7th; Autumn, whose element is Metal, falls between August 7th and November 7th; and Winter, whose element is Water, falls between November 7th and February 4th.

CREATE YOUR HEXAGRAM

You will need to use three coins to create your hexagram. Whether they are old Chinese coins or new Western coins, they must be of equal weight; three pennies will do. I keep three special coins just for consulting the *I Ching*. When you have selected your coins, run cold water over them for a while to clear them of other people's vibrations, then put the coins in a special place for safekeeping. Always approach the *I Ching* with respect and with the pure intention of discovering the truth.

When you wish to consult the *I Ching*, the first thing you need to do is formulate your question clearly and simply. With this method be sure to formulate your question so that the answer will be either yes or no. It is always a good practice to write down your question before you begin, and to fully concentrate on it while throwing your coins.

The way to throw your coins is as follows:

Take up your coins, and cup both of your hands around them. Shake the coins as you would dice, then drop them on a table, or on the floor if you are sitting on the floor.

Examine the combination of heads and tails your throw reveals. The values of the combinations are as follows:

- Two tails and one head equal a solid, or yang, line (——);
- Two heads and one tail equal a broken, or yin, line (— —);

- Three heads equal a changing yang line, for which you should draw a solid line with a circle over it (–◯–);
- Three tails equal a changing yin line, for which you should draw a broken line with an x over it (–x–).

The result of your first throw will constitute the first, bottom line of your hexagram. Draw this line on your paper. Take the three coins and repeat the process, keeping your question in mind, to obtain the second line of your hexagram. Then repeat the process, recording each throw, until you have obtained all six lines of your hexagram. Remember, hexagrams are always built from the bottom to the top.

CHANGING LINES

A hexagram with one or more changing lines (lines where you have superimposed either an *o* or an *x*), converts to a second hexagram with each changing line converting to its opposite. A changing yang line in your first hexagram converts to a yin line in your second hexagram, while a changing yin line in your first hexagram converts to a yang line in your second hexagram.

In the following example, line 2 is a changing yin line. This gives us a second hexagram whose second line becomes a yang line. Whenever you have a hexagram with changing lines, draw your second hexagram alongside your first.

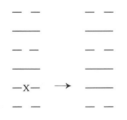

To find your hexagram number, note the lower trigram and the upper trigram of your hexagram, and refer to table 1: "Identifying the Hexagrams." Repeat this process for your second hexagram if there were changing lines in your first.

In table 1 the lower trigrams are listed in the left-hand column and the upper trigrams in the top row. The hexagram numbers are in the body of the table. You will find the number of your hexagram where the horizontal row, extending from your lower trigram meets the vertical column extending from your upper trigram. For example, if you obtained the hexagrams shown here, you will find that their numbers are 39 and 48. Write down the number of your hexagram (or hexagrams if there are changing lines).

```
 — —      — —
 ———      ———
 — —      — —
 ———      ———
—x—       ———
 — —      — —
 39        48
```

FINDING THE GROUP NUMBER OF YOUR HEXAGRAM

Noting the number of your hexagram, you will find its group number in table 2: "Hexagram Groups." Across the top of the table you will see the numbers 1 through 8. In the body of the table, you will see eight columns of numbers representing the sixty-four hexagrams. Find your hexagram's number. Then look at the number at the top of its column; this is the number of your hexagram's group.

Hexagram 39 (you will find the number 39 at the bottom of table 2, fifth in from the left) comes under group number 5. Please note, this step applies only to your original, or first, hexagram.

FINDING THE SIGNIFICATOR LINE

Noting the group number of your hexagram, refer now to table 3: "Significator Lines." The hexagram group numbers are listed across the top of the table. You will find your significator line number under your hexagram's group number. The number of your significator line refers to one of the lines in your hexagram.

Using the example of hexagram 39, which is in group 5, we find that line 4 is the significator line. Mark the significator line on your hexagram with an s.

```
      — —
      ———
  s   — —
      ———
    —x—
      — —
      39
```

FINDING THE ELEMENTS OF THE IMPORTANT LINES

Each line of any given hexagram has a corresponding element. The important lines of your hexagram are

- Your significator line
- Any changing lines in your first hexagram
- The converted lines in your second hexagram

Refer to table 4, "Corresponding Elements," to find the elements of each of these lines.

You will notice that table 4 consists of eight lower trigrams and eight upper trigrams. If your significator line or any changing line is in the lower trigram of your hexagram, find its corresponding element within the matching lower trigram in table 4. If your significator line or any changing line is in the upper trigram of your hexagram, find its corresponding element within the matching upper trigram in table 4.

Let's use our example of hexagram 39. We found that the significator line is line 4. Seeing that the fourth line is the bottom line in the upper trigram, we take the upper trigram and find its match in the third upper trigram in table 4. Because the significator line in our hexagram is the bottom line in the upper trigram, we find that the corresponding element of the significator line is Metal.

Now let's look at the changing second line in hexagram 39, and at the second line in hexagram 48, to which hexagram 39 converted. You will notice that the changing line, line 2, is in the middle of the lower trigram of hexagram 39. Take this trigram, and find its match in the fourth lower trigram in table 4. Because the changing line in our hexagram is the middle line in the lower trigram, we find that the corresponding element of the changing line is Fire. Next, following the same procedure, you will notice that the corresponding element of the middle line in the lower trigram of hexagram 48 is Water.

```
      — —                    — —
     ——————                 ——————
 s   — —    METAL           — —
     ——————                 ——————
     —x—     FIRE           —————— WATER
      — —                    — —
       39                     48
```

FINDING THE ANSWER

Now you are ready to use table 5, "Element Relations," to evaluate the lines in your hexagram. You will notice the five elements listed along the top row and down the left-hand column. The five elements along the top are subjects, and the five elements down the left-hand side are transformers. In the body of table 5 you will see the words "increases," "weakens," "exhausts," "kills," "supports." These words describe what the transformers do to the subjects. "Increases" and "supports" have favorable meanings, while "exhausts" and "kills" have unfavorable meanings. "Weakens" has a changeable, or uncertain meaning; it cautions.

Here is the three-step method for finding your answer. Of the three steps, the first is the most important. The second step modifies the first, and the third modifies the second.

STEP 1: Take the element of your significator line as the subject and the element of the season in which you are asking your question as the transformer. If, for example, the element of the significator line in your hexagram is Water and the element of the season in which you are asking your question is Metal, you have a yes answer, since the table indicates that Metal supports Water. Taking another example, if the element of your significator line is Fire and the element of the season is Metal, you have a no answer, since Metal exhausts Fire.

STEP 2: Take the element of your significator line as the subject and the element of the changing line in your original hexagram as the transformer. For example, if the element of your significator line is Water and you have a changing line whose element is Earth, the changing line threatens your significator line, since Earth kills Water. Taking another example, if the element of your significator line is Water and you have a changing line whose element is Metal, the changing line aids your significator line, since Metal supports Water.

STEP 3: Take the element of the changing line in your original hexagram as the subject and the element of the converted line in your second hexagram as the transformer. Building on the first example in step 2, where the element of the significator line was Water, and the element of the changing line was Earth, let's suppose that the element of the converted line is Wood. Because the Wood of the converted line kills the Earth of the changing line, the converted line cancels the destructive effect the changing line had on the significator line. If the element of the converted line had supported the element of the changing line, it would have reinforced the destructive power the changing line had over the significator line.

If your significator line is also a changing line, and this does occur from time to time, judge the element of the significator line first against the element of the season and second against the element of the significator's converted line in the second hexagram. Then, if there are other changing lines in the hexagram, judge the significator line against them.

Now let's take two examples of divinations. In the first example, the question is, "Will I obtain the funds I need?"

```
              — —                    SEASON ELEMENT
        S     — —   WATER                WATER
              — —
              ———
              — —
              — —
               15
```

First, noting the element of winter, the season in which this question was asked, and creating the hexagram, we have Water as the element of the season and hexagram 15. There are no changing lines. This makes the divination simple and straightforward. The fifth line is the significator line, and its element is Water. Since the Water of the significator line is increased by the Water of the season, the answer is yes.

Here is another divination. The question is, "Will you, dear reader, use this divination system to your advantage?"

```
—x—  WATER        ——— WOOD              SEASON ELEMENT
 —O— EARTH         — — WATER                WATER
 — —              — —
 — —              — —
s — — WOOD         — —
 —O— WATER         — — EARTH
  3
```

Noting the element of winter, the season in which this question was asked, and creating the hexagram, we have Water as the element of the season and hexagram 3 as our original hexagram. The second line of our hexagram is the significator line, and its element is Wood. Since the Wood of the significator line is supported by the Water of the season, the answer appears to be a clear yes.

Looking at the changing lines, we have two Waters and one Earth. The Waters add support to our significator while the Earth would exhaust it. Comparing the strength of the changing lines against their converted lines in the second hexagram, we can see that they are all compromised: the top line of the upper trigram, whose element is Water, is weakened by the Wood of its converted line; the middle line of the upper trigram, whose element is Earth, is exhausted by the Water of its converted line; and the bottom line of the lower hexagram, whose element is Water, is killed by the Earth of its converted line. Because the changing lines are so compromised, their effects on the significator line in our divination are made negligible. The answer to our question, therefore, is clearly yes. May this divination method point the way to success for you.

TABLE 1. IDENTIFYING THE HEXAGRAMS

UPPER ⟶ TRIGRAM / LOWER TRIGRAM ↓	Heaven	Thunder	Water	Mountain	Earth	Wind	Fire	Lake
Heaven	1	34	5	26	11	9	14	43
Thunder	25	51	3	27	24	42	21	17
Water	6	40	29	4	7	59	64	47
Mountain	33	62	39	52	15	53	56	31
Earth	12	16	8	23	2	20	35	45
Wind	44	32	48	18	46	57	50	28
Fire	13	55	63	22	36	37	30	49
Lake	10	54	60	41	19	61	38	58

TABLE 2. HEXAGRAM GROUPS

GROUP NUMBER	1	2	3	4	5	6	7	8
HEXAGRAM NUMBERS	1	44	33	12	20	23	35	14
	29	60	3	63	49	55	36	7
	52	22	26	41	38	10	61	53
	51	16	40	32	46	48	28	17
	57	9	37	42	25	21	27	18
	30	56	50	64	4	59	6	13
	2	24	19	11	34	43	5	8
	58	47	45	31	39	15	62	54

TABLE 3. SIGNIFICATOR LINES

Group Number	1	2	3	4	5	6	7	8
Significator Line	6	1	2	3	4	5	4	3

TABLE 4. CORRESPONDING ELEMENTS

Trigram	1	2	3	4
upper	— Earth — Metal — Fire	– – Earth – – Metal — Fire	– – Water — Earth – – Metal	— Wood – – Water – – Earth
lower	— Earth — Wood — Water	– – Earth – – Wood — Water	– – Fire — Earth – – Wood	— Metal – – Fire – – Earth

Trigram	5	6	7	8
upper	– – Metal – – Water – – Earth	— Wood — Fire – – Earth	— Fire – – Earth — Metal	– – Earth — Metal — Water
lower	– – Wood – – Fire – – Earth	— Metal — Water – – Earth	— Water – – Earth — Wood	– – Earth — Wood — Fire

TABLE 5. ELEMENT RELATIONS

Subject	Wood	Fire	Earth	Metal	Water
Transformer					
Wood	Increases	Supports	Kills	Exhausts	Weakens
Fire	Weakens	Increases	Supports	Kills	Exhausts
Earth	Exhausts	Weakens	Increases	Supports	Kills
Metal	Kills	Exhausts	Weakens	Increases	Supports
Water	Supports	Kills	Exhausts	Weakens	Increases

THE TALISMANS

The talismans were painted by the award-winning calligrapher and seal engraver Zeng Xianwen, a fellow of the Chinese Academy of the Arts and a member of many other calligraphers' associations.

Born into a distinguished and ancient family of scholars in Jinzhou in southern Liaoning and now residing in the United States, Zeng Xianwen has had his works featured in numerous publications and art exhibitions in China and has been selected for inclusion in "Beijing 2000 Olympics: First International Exhibition of Painting and Calligraphy." His works of calligraphy are in the collections of several museums. He has been named by the Chinese government an Art Talent Treasure.

1. PROTECTION

2. PEACE

3. WOOD

4. METAL

5 . FIRE

6. EARTH

7. WATER

8. PROSPERITY

9. VICTORY

INDEX